between
black
and
white

GROWING UP
BROWN IN
APARTHEID
SOUTH AFRICA

A MEMOIR

GANESAN ABBU

The author at age 2 with his parents and baby brother, Poobal (Circa-1965)

Copyrighted Material
The use of any part of this publication, reproduced, transmitted in any form or by any means, electronically, mechanical, photocopying, recording or otherwise, or stored in a retrieval system without the prior written consent of the publisher would constitute an infringement of the copyright law.

Copyright C 2023 by Ganesan Abbu
All rights reserved

Published by: Ganesan Abbu Publishing Corporation

Name: Ganesan Abbu
Title: Between Black and White

ISBN: 978-1-7389531-0-3 (Paperback)
ISBN: 978-1-7389531-2-7 (Hardcover)
ISBN: 978-1-7389531-1-0 (ebook)

Cover Design: Damonza
Layout: Damonza

First Edition

Between Black and White is a work of non fiction. The author has no intention to offend, malign, or bring into disrepute any individual, groups of individuals, organization, or country. The timeframes of certain events may have been changed to keep the narrative discourse in context. Some names and identifying details have been changed.

For my children,

Tharunamaya, Kavithan, and Diviyani.

May this reminder of your roots guide your paths into the future!

Table of Contents

Chapter 1: An Awful Time to Be Born 1
Chapter 2: Coolie be gone. 10
Chapter 3: Locked in Indenture 22
Chapter 4: The Roots of My Ambition 30
Chapter 5: Lost in Translation 41
Chapter 6: A Whitewashed Education. 51
Chapter 7: 1949. 61
Chapter 8: The Risk of Ruin 71
Chapter 9: A Crisis of Conscience. 86
Chapter 10: The Social Experiment. 99
Chapter 11: My Textbook of Learning 114
Chapter 12: A Complicated Relationship. 125
Chapter 13: The Maharajah and the Sepoys 136
Chapter 14: An Ethical Dilemma. 147
Chapter 15: Agent of Change 158
Chapter 16: The Dream Comes Together 171
Chapter 17: Things Fall Apart 182
Chapter 18: Canada Calls 193
Chapter 19: A Child of the Universe. 198

between
black
and
white

CHAPTER 1

An Awful Time to Be Born

It was an awful time to be born in South Africa, especially for a Brown boy in a world that was Black and White. There was quite a frenzy, that October night in 1962, as Mom unexpectedly went into labor. Dad rushed off in the dark to fetch the midwife. I picture him now, with a pounding heart and a Viceroy cigarette nervously fluttering in his mouth, half walking, half running, striking a match to ward off the snapping dogs.

This was a grim time to be starting a life. In those first moments—as I was held upside down by the ankles, coughing and spluttering in the dawn of apartheid, dangling precariously over smoke that rose above the *sambrani* (frankincense) sprinkled over glowing coals—I had no idea about my hazy future in a segregated South Africa, my tenuous position as an Indian person in this society, and the doubts that would arise as to where I really belonged.

Several days later, a Hindu priest was summoned and given the precise time and date of my birth. He studied the astrological charts and bestowed upon me a name that resonated with the stars. That is how I came to be called Ganesan, in honor of the elephant god, Ganesha, who represents wisdom and clears all obstacles.

My birth-certificate labelled me as 'Indian'. The sequence of my genes, over which I exerted no choice or control, coded into me the physical attributes that were used to construct my racial identity: brown skin, brown eyes, and straight black hair. In case these characteristics were not self-evident, when I was older I had to produce upon demand an identity card that confirmed my race.

My identity document was the stamp that determined the trajectory of my life. The law said that I could only live amongst people who looked like me and spoke like me. To live alongside people of another race, attend school with them, or socialize with them was against the regulations. We were not allowed to sit on a park bench beside White people, swim on the same beach, or travel on the same bus. The Immorality Act strictly forbade anyone from marrying across the color line. Even in sickness and in death we were separated, restricted to either White or non-White hospitals and racially-segregated cemeteries. It was as though the corpses would rise unnoticed and, in some ghoulish dance, transgress the laws of the land. There was no choice, no chance to alter this course. It was the law.

It was indeed a terrible time to be born. South Africa had just declared itself a republic and the blueprint for apartheid was being shaped. Since 1913 colonial Britain had established a system of territorial separation that maintained a divide between White and non-White individuals. A new Afrikaner-dominated Nationalist government began to build upon the foundation of British policies and entrench racial segregation into law. The Population Registration Act officially separated people into one of four racial categories that was based mainly on the color of one's skin.

African, Asian, and 'Coloured' (mixed-race) people were being shuffled around like pieces on a Rubik's cube. A grand plan—executed under The Group Areas Act—ensured that residential areas were inhabited only by people with the same skin color. There was no regard for who was the rightful owner of the land, how attached one was to a place, or what emotional ties existed between people who shared that common space. Prime locations with oceanfront views and urban business centers were reserved exclusively for White-skinned people. African people were forced into newly-constructed townships on the outskirts of urban centers or driven into distant rural 'homelands' called *Bantustans*. Indian and Coloured people were strategically positioned in residential areas that acted as buffer zones shielding White people from the African Townships. An entire province, the Orange Free State, was set aside for White people only. It held nothing orange, nor was it free. I would need a special permit to transit through this area.

Six months before I was born, our family home was in the village of Old Duffs Road. I'm not sure of the real name, but that's what my grandparents called it. It was on the outskirts of Durban, a coastal city on the eastern seaboard of South Africa, where almost 90 percent of South Africa's one million Indians lived.

Old Duffs Road was a lively and somewhat uncommon place, where Indian and African people shared a communal area. The fireworks that illuminated the night sky during the Hindu celebration of Diwali, the Muslim *azan* (call to prayer) at 5 a.m., and the rhythmic notes of the *izimbomu* (a ceremonial horn used by the African Shembe Church) were celebrated equally by all who lived there. The community was very poor, but they shared the little they had. Our family sent dried fish chutney and rice to their African neighbor. They liked the spicy flavors. They would reciprocate with *phutu*, a crumbly maize porridge.

Before it was an edict, it was a rumor. I imagine my grandparents craning to hear the news. They want to do what? Demolish our homes! Panicked messages race through the village. People mill about a notice from the *Government Gazette*, some weep, and others stare with blank expressions.

"You must remove all your belongings and leave your premises within the next seven days," the notice reads.

"Will they really force us out?" I imagine my grandfather saying.

"They can't be so cruel," my grandmother replies.

Then, on the seventh day, the community is startled awake by blaring sirens and the grinding groan of bulldozers. My grandfather rushes outside. His neighbors are already gathered there, imploring the policemen to see reason.

"I have an order of the court," one of them says. It was the only license he needed.

The police stood guard with rifles in hand as my family packed some clothes, a few photographs, and a single pot into an old Mazza rice bag.

Bulldozers set about with annihilating persistence—crushing, dragging, and tearing their homes to bits. By nightfall there was only a blanketing silence, a silence that echoed the grief of those freshly dispossessed of their homes. Gone were the crudely scratched-out triangles, rectangles, and circles where my mother had once played hopscotch in her childhood. Gone were the girlish alternations of timidity and petulance, of tears and playful laughter, that accompanied a missed jump or an awkward hop. Gone was the temple where my father did more than the required three rounds, just so that he could get another glimpse of my mother, who lived next door. Gone, too, was the blush on Mom's teenage face—while she rocked an imaginary doll fashioned out of a rolled towel and watched him do the rounds. Only the debris of flattened buildings kept company with the dust and the haze that filled the air.

Another piece of the Rubik's Cube clicked into place. My family was tossed across the railway tracks, into an area designated for Indian people. Eventually the compensation that was paid to them—all of one hundred pounds—was only enough to purchase a dustbowl plot of land in the new Duffs Road.

They lived like squatters in makeshift dwellings that were hastily put together from scraps of tin and pieces of wood. Over time my family joined together with other families and pooled their skills and resources. One brick at a time they tried to fashion some semblance of a normal existence. Slowly they rebuilt their homes, their lives, and their self-respect. For months, if not years, as much as they tried to move forward they were held back by a lingering sense of loss.

My family had never expected this, had never seriously considered the seven-day ultimatum to leave. They believed blindly that by some miracle, by some divine intervention, the authorities would not follow through. Within a few hours, their land, their home, and their dignity were all crushed by a decree that was a few miserable words scrawled on a crumpled piece of paper. There was no recourse, no power to challenge the many hands that were complicit in carrying out such a large-scale injustice: White politicians who wrote such measures into law, senior White officials who curated the bureaucratic fine print, an entire court system that was controlled by White people, who, together with White policemen, enforced the rules.

All over the country, people of color were on the move, dispossessed of their land and displaced within their own country. The chaos served only the interest of a misdirected ideology, which the Afrikaner people called *apartheid*.

It was as though a crazy farmer had a dream, and in that dream, God appeared before him and placed in his hand four magical seeds. The seeds, he was told, had the power to influence a new reality, a dreamworld of sorts in which the seed would determine the destiny of each racial group: where they lived, what types of schools they attended, and what resources they would have. And the farmer believed that God had intended things to be this way, separate but unequal, and that god had entrusted *him*, the White farmer, with the responsibility of deciding how each of these magical seeds would be assigned. And so it was that the worst seed was given to the majority race, and that they were left to the mercy of a bleak future. The seed that offered the best of everything the farmer kept for his own kind; and the in-between seed varieties he left to the two racial groups that were in between.

Afrikaner people believed in their hearts that they could correctly organize society by using neutral physical differences such as skin color as the basis for ranking human value. However, at its core, apartheid was designed to ensure the social and economic dominance of White people. The system's fictitious gradations were designed to extinguish any sense of common humanity, and fixed bleak boundaries to the lives of all those who were not White.

Life was most harsh for African people. They were not allowed to own property or businesses in the urban centers and were pushed into the barren landscape of the rural 'homelands'.

African labor, though, was crucial to the success of White business interests. The laborers, who were almost exclusively men, were housed in inner-city hostels and provided with permits they called *dompasses*. The *dompasses* specified where African people could work or travel to. They had to show these documents to policemen whose job it was to randomly check on such things. Forgetting to carry the *dompass*, misplacing it, or having it stolen rendered one liable to arrest and imprisonment. The system of migrant labor fractured the family structure. Women and children were left to fend for themselves in the homelands, where there was no work, and where poverty was rife, and disease prevailed.

Indian traders were allowed to function in restricted areas within the urban landscape. They acted as middlemen between White wholesalers and the African majority customers. Perhaps it was just chance, or maybe it was designed exactly in that manner, but Indian people were wedged into the middle, between White people and African people.

In the face of such injustice, one may rightly enquire as to why African people, who outnumbered White people by four to one, did not stand up and defend their rights.

In what was effectively a police state, the African National Congress was active as an underground movement. In August of 1962, just two months prior to my birth, Nelson Mandela was arrested and detained about an hour's drive northwest of Durban. There had been widespread resistance to forced removals, but an unarmed people, however strong in number, could not match the well-armed machinery of the state.

To understand the context of our subjugation, one has to appreciate that our troubles were rooted in a chequered history that went back three hundred years.

In the fifteenth century the insatiable European appetite for spices from Java, Sumatra, and India was one of the driving forces behind the Voyages of Discovery. When the overland trade route through Europe was cut off by the war between the Christians and the Moors, it became imperative to find a sea route to the East. This quest saw Christopher Columbus sailing across the Atlantic Ocean and stumbling upon America. The Portuguese were the first of many seafaring nations to travel down the west coast of Africa, around its southern tip at the Cape of Storms, and all the way up the East African coast towards India. However, the Portuguese did not see any benefit from colonizing South Africa.

In primary school our history textbooks taught us that the Cape was discovered by the colonizing powers. One of the dates that is indelibly inscribed in the minds of all South African students is April 6, 1652. That was the day when Jan van Riebeeck arrived at the Cape and set up a halfway house for the Dutch East India Company: a refreshment station that would stave off the deadly scurvy and provide the sailors with reprieve from the 'Cape of Storms.'

They *arrived*. The land was *waiting*. Empty and waiting. The simple act of arriving was all that was required to lay claim to a land that was waiting, *waiting* for a selected people to *arrive* and assert ownership. It did not matter that the Khoi people had inhabited those lands ten thousand years earlier, and that those lands held for them a vibrant history and culture that was filled with deep spiritual meaning.

The story of dispossession is ultimately a story of people and the enduring legacies of injustice. How better to create a pretext—to justify dominance over those made landless and secure a future that favored imperialistic intentions—than to deny a people's ancient past and characterize them as unworthy of holding any rights to the land. 'Strandlopers,' that was how the Dutch portrayed the Khoi: godless savages and beasts, who foraged and scavenged on the beach for food.

The slender bows and stone-tipped arrows of the Khoi were no match for the muskets and cannons of the Dutch. Life on the southern tip of Africa—where the cold Atlantic and warm Indian Oceans meet—looked favorably on the Dutch, who now heralded the Cape of Storms as the Cape of Good Hope.

Where power grows out of the barrel of a gun, the one with a bigger gun, a more powerful cannon, is sure to wrest control and exert dominance. Two hundred years later the British recognized the strategic maritime position of the Cape. Encouraged also by the discovery of gold and diamonds in South Africa, they defeated the Dutch in the Anglo-Boer Wars. It would take two wars, the second fought over three years, to entrench British influence in South Africa. More than a century and a half later I was cast into this world in which the Afrikaner nation—the descendants of the Dutch explorers—had just regained their dominance. They were busy entrenching their influ- ence, re-establishing their pride, and making absolutely sure that the mistakes of the past were never to be repeated.

The essential character of three hundred years of suppression, first by colonization and then by apartheid, was that people of color were not free to choose in South Africa, but had a social structure that was forced upon them. In the innocence of my early childhood these false divisions appeared as though they were the natural order of things. I trusted all that I saw and experienced, believed without question that the circumstances under which I lived were the way that life was intended, accepted without reason that I belonged in this place, and assumed without proof that Indian people had always been a part of South Africa.

Exploring my experiences during apartheid in South Africa made me challenge the misconceptions that I held in my childhood.

However, it would take many years for me to understand the truth of it, and those years would be fraught with struggle. I came to realize how difficult it was to be sandwiched between African people and White people, what an ordeal it would be to unshackle myself from the constraints of apartheid, and how, through this journey, I would constantly question the notion of where I really belonged.

CHAPTER 2

Coolie be gone.

I spent most of my early childhood in the village of Duffs Road. Our little hamlet lay on a sharp bend in the road that led from Durban toward the African township of Kwa Mashu. In the arc of that road was a factory that assembled bus body frames onto chassis. Next to the body shop was a row of businesses: a general store, a barber shop, and a funeral parlor. There were many accidents on that bend, and survivors often claimed that they saw ghosts and heard eerie, unexplained voices. People in our village often joked that accident victims had a good chance of ending up in either the body shop or the funeral home.

The houses in our village were mostly modest dwellings, made from bricks or blocks and covered in plaster. Many homes were painted in pastel shades that reminded me of ice cream. Our house was banana yellow and our next-door neighbors' strawberry pink and lime green. The family that made their fortune in the bus assembly enterprise lived in palatial buildings that were shaped like monuments to the transport industry: ships, buses, and even airplanes. The airplane house came complete with a glass-windowed cockpit that served as a viewing deck, wings that were constructed to scale, and a fuselage adapted into living quarters.

We lived in an extended family dwelling on Swan Road, only three doors away from the bus factory. My younger brother Poobal and I shared a cramped two-bedroom home with our parents, paternal grandparents, and my father's younger brother and sister. It was remarkable how we managed with so little space.

Only Indian people were allowed to live in Duffs Road. I spent the first two or three years of my life in this insular bubble, sealed off from the outside and surrounded only by people who looked like me, dressed like me, and spoke like me. If you walked through the streets you would have noticed the rich and diverse tapestry of traditions that gave clues to who we were. You would have spotted the warm glow of freshly-strung marigold garlands draped above our front door. It was typical of the welcoming entranceway to any Tamil-speaker's home. The red flags hoisted on bamboo poles (*jhanda*) outside our neighbor's house would have given you a clue that my three friends who lived there spoke Hindustani.

I knew of no other world outside of Duffs Road and I felt safe in this cocooned existence that was sheltered from everything that lay outside. My earliest recollection of venturing outside this cloistered existence was when I was four years old.

On a hot summer's night during the Christmas period of 1966 we were driving along the Golden Mile. This is a long stretch of beachfront road that lies about ten kilometers away from Duffs Road. The Golden Mile was Durban's answer to Copacabana in Rio, or South Beach, Miami.

Tropical was certainly the dominant aura on the Golden Mile. It was lined with grand colonial-style hotels that were surrounded by clipped green lawns, and fringed with palm trees. It was a storybook setting, something in between the glamour and glitz of *The Great Gatsby* and an enchanting fairy-tale world. White men in dinner jackets and their ladies in polka-dot dresses dined on the verandahs of elegant restaurants. Attentive Indian waiters in black pants and crisp white coats decanted wine, carved meat, and poured sauces with white-gloved hands.

We drove along the Golden Mile, Mom and Dad up front and Poobal and me in the back seat of our second-hand blue Vauxhall. I turned down the window, stuck out my nose, and savored the misty, charcoal-grilled flavors that were infused with the salty sprays blowing off surfers' paradise. I longed to know what those diners were eating, so I concocted my own ideal menu based on delicacies that we could afford on special occasions: lamb chops from the Top Market butcher, the tender breast meat of a Cornish hen, and jumbo pink prawns fresh from the waters off Lourenço Marques.

Although we were forbidden to dine at the restaurants or join in the fun, we were allowed to walk along the promenade. Finding parking was particularly difficult during the summer, a time when hordes of White vacationers came down from the interior for their annual pilgrimage to the ocean. We had to go around several times, and each time I urged Dad to drive as slowly as possible, secretly wishing for every traffic light to turn red. Dad eased back, fired up a cigarette with the dashboard lighter, stuck his elbow out of the window, and went around the block. There was a moment when we double parked, but a hulking police officer on foot patrol thumped on the roof and we moved forward with a little lurch and a jolt and set off on yet another trip around the block. We finally found parking in some poorly-lit back street, far away from the main hub of activity.

I was truly mesmerized, wide eyed, open mouthed, and bouncing about with excitement as we strolled along the Golden Mile that night. I parted the hedge and leant forward to get a better look into the wonderland on the ocean side. There were children everywhere, frolicking in the paddling pools, running about with ice cream cones, and some riding the chair-lift cableway above. A larger-than-life rendition of the beloved nursery-rhyme figure Mother Goose—wearing a blue pinafore apron and cradling a basket filled with a delightful floral arrangement—stood dotingly over her goslings.

After watching the people who were eating in those fancy restaurants, I felt a sense of inadequacy and inferiority. I secretly hoped that someday I would be able to enjoy the same level of luxury. A surge of yearning washed over me, a force so powerful that even feelings of inadequacy could not be contained.

"I want to play in the water with those children, Dad," I said.

Dad put his arm around my shoulder, "The police won't let you, son. You must wear a bathing costume to play there," he said.

"I'll take off my shorts and go in my underpants," I said.

"No," Dad said, using a tone that was much firmer. "We don't have towels. We'll come back another day."

"Let's get toffee apples or candied popcorn," said Mom.

I looked at the vendor who was walking about with a tray strapped around his neck. Those treats look good, I thought; but now that Mom's guard was down I could bargain for more. I strutted along with the chocolate-covered Eskimo Pie, and Poobal got the multi-colored umbrella ice cream.

The Golden Mile was a magical place, a fantasy world that was in our world and yet not in *my* world, locked away and inaccessible like some faraway land. Over time I came to understand that the excuses Mom and Dad made, their bartering, the distractions, and even the threats, were intended to teach us about what was permissible and what was not. Our parents were shielding us from the storms of evil misfortune that racism brings upon children, preparing us for the day when we too would come face to face with racism.

A month later, in January of 1967, I came to experience life on the outside in a way that was more up close and personal. The actual events, like most things for someone who is only four, remain only as fragments in my memory. However, there are some moments that I recall with absolute clarity.

Living in an extended family lent itself to a level of pampering that at times bordered on the ridiculous. As a baby I was handed over from one set of arms to another, and wailed uncontrollably whenever I was set down. Perhaps this explains how, even as a four-year-old, Ayah was carrying me on her hip whilst feeding me that Friday night.

Ayah, my paternal grandmother, added a dollop of butter to soft-boiled rice and dhal. Then she rolled the mixture into bite-sized balls. She placed each morsel into my mouth, one ball at a time. Ayah had the habit of turning the last handful a divine three times around my head before feeding it to me. On that particular evening, and despite her repeated attempts, I refused the last helping.

Ayah would have none of that. "*Bululu bamba* will carry you off in a sack," she said, resorting to a common threat in 'Fanagalo,' a Zulu-based pidgin language. Even the threat of a young African man carrying me off in a sack could not gain my compliance. In a last attempt to convince me to finish my meal, Ayah made an offer that I couldn't refuse.

"If you finish your food, you can go to town with Thatha," she promised, referring to my grandfather, who was taking the train the following day. I finished my meal with newfound willingness. Ayah cracked her knuckles on the sides of her head and exclaimed, "*Amada*!" which means 'Beloved!' in Tamil.

The next morning, I jumped out of bed early because we were running on Thatha's time. He was always up and ready for the day by 5:30. Ayah pulled a handkerchief out of her apron pocket, untied a corner, and retrieved a folded one rand note.

"For you," she said as she placed it in my palm.

With that, Thatha and I made our way towards the train station, which was situated on the opposite end of Duffs Road and adjacent to the African township of Kwa Mashu.

We descended the stairs onto the platform at the train station. There was a large white signboard that proudly announced the altitude at Duffs Road: 88 ft. We passed by a charming little building with baskets of brightly-colored flowers that hung from the rafters. A large, sand-filled red bucket was attached to the wall. A room full of polished wooden benches caught my eye. I could not read the sign outside, but I would see a similar one later that day: *Net Blankes* (Whites only).

We hurried towards the far end of the platform, rushing past empty carriages, and squeezed into a third-class compartment. A sharp whistle cut through the air as the doors slammed shut behind us. Suddenly I found myself surrounded by African men, not just one or two, but what seemed like hundreds of *bululu bambas*. I shook with fear, nauseated by a definite sense of danger.

I found it perplexing how Thatha managed to maintain such composure throughout it all. Watching him chat with some of the men in the Zulu language was reassuring. Somewhat reassuring.

We entered a short tunnel and my apprehension returned. Instead of relief, the emerging light sent shivers down my spine. A strange and intimidating man appeared. He wore a crown of horns and a goatskin skirt adorned with beaded tassels that swayed and jangled with the movement of the train. Each rattle and shake sent the tassels flailing like the tentacles of an octopus that threatened to ensnare me. I clung tightly onto Thatha and closed my eyes. This must be the very man Ayah had warned me about, the one who carries off disobedient children who refuse to finish their meals. The thought of being trapped inside a sack was overwhelming, and for a moment I felt like thrashing about to break free from the coach.

Upon our reaching the station in Durban, Thatha took my hand and fixed his attention firmly ahead. My gaze wandered eagerly over the curious sights that had captured my interest: pigeons strutting through well-manicured gardens, towering palm trees, and the domes, arches, and pillars of grand and unfamiliar buildings. More than anything I was intrigued that most people in this area were 'European.' (My family referred to all White people as European and Black people as African.)

There were many White people on the Golden Mile, but it was night and I had seen them from afar. I felt like Alice through the looking glass, experiencing at once the fascination and uncertainty of looking out from inside a mirror and into a strange new world.

We entered a tall building with giant glass entrance doors. A European lady sat at the door. She was a slender woman with brown curls, a long face with red lipstick, and a pointed chin. Her stockinged legs were gracefully draped over a tall wooden stool.

"*Hierso* (Here)," she said, and without even raising her head, she pointed us towards a long line of people, continuing to buff her nails. I was impressed that she knew exactly where we needed to go. We had not asked, and there were shorter lines with only a few European people, but she directed us towards a sign that read, *Nie Blankes* (Non-Whites). My tiny legs were weakened from all that standing and waiting. Finally it was our turn. Thatha presented his identity card, placed his right thumb print on a form, and handed over some money for the electricity bill.

I struggled to keep up with Thatha, who was striding along Smith Street and encouraging a linear trajectory. Then suddenly, I stopped. Standing before me was a European boy, slender and blonde-haired, who appeared to be about my height. My gaze met his for just a moment, and in the depths of his bright blue eyes, I saw a reflection that appeared to mirror the same curiosity and confusion that I was feeling. Perhaps my gaze had turned into a stare, loitering in ways that were misconstrued. I could not prevent them from lingering, from inquisitively surveying the little details that I was drawn to. He was not like any of the children I had grown up around. I couldn't help myself, for I had never seen a European child from such close range.

I hadn't noticed, but the boy's mother was standing beside him. In one fell swoop, she yanked him around and pierced me with a dagger-like stare. I was not sure where her sense of threat was coming from, but it was there: I could feel it, and it was strong.

"Bloody Coolies, go back where you came from," she shouted.

So, there we were, Thatha and I, in the middle of the street, stunned by the lady's outburst. What was I to believe, other than I had done something terribly wrong? I had offered what I thought to be a greeting of kindness, but my joy was slashed, and I was asked to go back to some place where I had come from.

"Sorry, ma'am," Thatha apologized.

Now, even though I could not grasp the meaning of his apology, I felt the interior charge of impropriety—convinced that I was guilty, that I had been in the wrong place, made a childish blunder, or broken some important rule.

"Why is the lady so angry, Thatha?" He remained silent.

"Why is she asking us to go back to Duffs Road?" Silence.

"What's a Coolie, Thatha?" I asked instead.

Even though he was a gentle man, Thatha seemed unnaturally strong in that moment, his grip on my arm almost painful. Lurking just beyond that irritation was something more, something troubling, a rising fury perhaps.

Some of the passers-by turned sharply about and began to stare at us, whilst others halted outright and laughed. Thatha pulled me away and we marched on without looking back.

There was no doubt that Thatha was in a tough spot. I felt he was holding back and not standing up to her, as though there was some danger in speaking up. To a sensitive child, it was troubling to see a grown man being treated so shabbily, and by a woman who was likely half his age. I plodded on silently, nursing contempt for the cruel lady.

When we were some safe distance away, Thatha finally responded.

"Coolie is a bad word," he muttered, "a very bad word."

At the intersection of Grey and Queen Streets, the entrance to Durban's Little India, order was restored. We were greeted by the calming fragrance of incense and the aroma of freshly-ground cumin, coriander, and cardamon. The trail of spice led down through a narrow alleyway and to an emporium that sold mounds of every variety of red chili powder. Some of the varietals' names indicated scorn for the most vilified familial category: mother-in-law's tongue, mother-in-law's hellfire, and mother-in-law exterminator. The arcade presented specialty stores: an Indian sari boutique with elegantly poised white manikins that were draped in exotic silks threads, a jewelry store with glittering windows filled with ornate twenty-two carat gold wedding sets, a tailor's shop with a cotton reel that bobbed up and down as the tailor pedaled his Singer sewing machine, and a record store that beat out the Beach Boys' *Good Vibrations*. There were also those stores that were crammed with a little bit of everything: shoes, leather bags, watches, children's clothes, electrical appliances, hair dye, and false hairpieces.

The sidewalk was filled with the vibrant chatter of buyers and sellers, of old friends catching up, and a one-legged beggar mechanically shaking his tin cup. Young Indian boys shouted out their wares, beckoning African customers into their stores with the call of "*Ngena phakathi, ngena phakhathi* (Come in, come in)."

The streets, too, were a torrent of activity. Rivers of vibrantly-colored people flowed unendingly, swirling around impatient drivers who bared their shark-like teeth as they attempted to turn across another tide of pedestrians. An *umfaan* (a young African boy) strained through the crowd, his cart overburdened with huge hessian sacks of rice.

All that commotion ought to have worked painfully on a young child's overwrought nerves, yet I felt a certain lightness, a calm, a feeling that this was where I belonged. It all seemed so natural and welcoming.

We stopped outside G. C. Kapitan's, the renowned Indian cafe on Durban's Grey Street. My eyes were immediately drawn to the magnificent displays of diamond-shaped sweetmeats, encrusted with slivered almonds and pistachios, and a towering heap of *jalebis*. We were promptly shown to a table by the window, overlooking the bustling street. Waiters moved deftly between tables, balancing plates of piping hot samoosas and chili-bites on their upturned palms. The air was filled with the rich aroma of spicy curry, while the sounds of sizzling savories emanated from the kitchen.

An aproned Indian waiter approached us, removed the pencil that was cradled above his ear, and stood ready with notepad in hand.

"What you want, uncle?"

Thatha dropped his right elbow on the table and leaned his chin onto his curled fingers, adopting a pose like Rodin's "The Thinker." Then he raised his head and said, "We'll have a quarter beans, sonny." There was no need to mention the item as listed in the menu: 'bunny chow.' It was understood.

A quarter bunny chow lay on a plate before us. It was bread, about six slices in depth but uncut, with the soft core scooped out to create a makeshift bowl. The sugar-bean curry that filled the hollowed center was steaming hot. I picked up a piece of the soft inner core, which was lying like a tilted cap on top of the curry, and dipped it into the gravy. It was still piping hot, so I had to blow on it before placing it into my mouth. From the opposite side, Thatha tore away at the crust and spooned up the curry from the well-soaked center.

It was a famous dish, this bunny chow. I learned that day that bunny chow had nothing to do with rabbits, its name arising from the corruption of a term that refers to the Indian merchant-class *Bunya* clan, whose restaurants first introduced the dish. It was uncanny that we never ate bunny chow at home. Yet it was easy enough to make, and the convenience of an edible container meant that there were no dishes to wash.

I felt a sense of satisfaction as I shared my first bunny chow with Thatha. For a brief moment I savored the thought of how jealous Poobal would be when I returned home and recounted the experience. I reached into my pocket and pulled out the one rand note that Ayah had given me. Gesturing to Thatha, I suggested that he buy Poobal some *boondhi,* sweet chickpea flour balls deep-fried and dipped in a syrupy orange solution. Thatha refused the money but went ahead and ordered the treat.

I looked out of the window, my attention arrested by the frenzy of impatient activity on the street outside. It looked much like a silent Charlie Chaplin pantomime, with the actors in flailing, staccato-like motions. The script, however, was as detached from slapstick comedy as day is from night.

I tensed up, my eyes became wide, and my heart raced. I clutched Thatha's hands and drew myself up in my chair. Though I was afraid and did not know precisely what I was going to see, I prepared for something extraordinary,

A White policeman appeared to be arresting a young African man. I feared that at any moment the policeman's raised truncheon would crash down upon the man's head. The man offered no resistance as the policeman grabbed him by his collar and shoved him into the caged back of the police van.

Another officer seemed to be questioning a balding, grey-bearded African man. The old man, who must have been about Thatha's age, was rummaging through his pockets, searching in his jacket and pants, emptying them out as though he had lost something important. Then the old man dropped slowly to his knees and put his hands together in prayer. The policeman shook his head disapprovingly, grabbed the man, and shoved him into the back of the police van.

The back of the police van was full, packed with African people who were caged in like animals. Some of their fingers hooked onto the mesh metal siding, their eyes vacant and staring out into a blank world.

I was at an age when I feared the police. Our parents invoked their name to command our compliance. "The police will catch you. They'll lock you up," they told us. Whenever I saw a police van go by on our street, I hid behind the curtains. I feared the police even more than I feared *bululu bambas*.

Their royal-blue uniforms, truncheons, and pistols were all instruments of power and authority. Therefore I believed without question that those crammed into the back of the police van had committed some crime, that they were prisoners. What else was I to believe?

Yet I needed confirmation, some explanation of what they had done. I looked earnestly towards Thatha, scrutinizing his face, hoping that I would uncover some clue that would satisfy my curiosity. He appeared detached and not in the least bothered by all that I had witnessed.

Finally I asked, "Why are the policemen locking them up, Thatha?"

He answered without emotion, "They did not have their *dompass* ('stupid pass', in Afrikaans). They must have a pass to be in the city."

"Where's our *dompass*, Thatha?" I asked, the plight of the people in the back of the police van becoming more evident as I began to understand their situation in terms of my own vulnerability.

"We don't need one," he said.

As much as I tried, the whirling ideas that chased one another in my four-year-old brain confused me profoundly. We did not need a *dompass*, therefore we must belong here. But the lady on the street demanded that we go back to where we came from. So, we must not belong here. We belonged, and we did not belong. How could that be?

CHAPTER 3

Locked in Indenture

Back then, when I was just four years old: I didn't really know what apartheid meant. Even though I witnessed people being arrested because they didn't have their *dompasses*, I didn't fully understand the significance of the rules and how they were enforced. For weeks, I couldn't stop thinking about the lady I saw on the street: how angry she got, how difficult it was for her to control herself, the way she insinuated that we didn't belong here, and how she screamed that we should go back to where we came from. All those thoughts stuck with me, like rain hanging in a cloud.

An entire week had passed since my first visit to town, and on a hot summer's night in January of 1967 Poobal and I lay cradled in Thatha's arms. All three of us—dressed in matching, striped shorty pajamas and fishnet vests—lay flat on our backs on a worn-out blanket that was spread over the bare ground beneath a giant syringa tree. The intense heat of the day had subsided, but the air remained heavy and humid. We gazed upwards to the heavens as the curtain of the night was drawn apart to reveal the splendor of the Milky Way.

Dad never used those exact words, but he once told me that a long time ago there was an explosion in the universe that caused the stars to form and scatter into space. His estimation about the birth of the cosmos might have had some mistakes, but that idea stuck with me. All that sparked my curiosity, and since that time I have been fascinated by the mysteries that fill the night sky.

As I gazed upwards, I tried my best to imagine the stars zooming away at incredible speeds; but everything seemed still, except for the slow rise of the full moon along the horizon. I could not help but be drawn to it, and was transported into a strange and dreamy state.

"Thatha, did we come from the moon?" I blurted out.

Maybe it was the perfect moment Thatha had been waiting for. That night, he shared with us the story of how our family and other Indian people ended up in South Africa. He seemed to remember every detail with remarkable clarity and precision, just like his father had told him.

The moonlight reflected off the three bold stripes of ashes on Thatha's forehead. He turned onto his side and cradled his head in the triangle formed by his bent elbow and wrist. Poobal and I inclined our heads to match his familiar pose. We were ripe with anticipation, our usual thoughts of black mambas entwining in the branches above, or centipedes curling up around our toes, unable to distract us.

Thatha's story began in the late 1800s when the British controlled most of the Indian subcontinent, including the Madras Presidency on the eastern seaboard. These were hard times in our motherland. The monsoons never came that year, or the next. The area was stricken by famine, and when the rains finally came, instead of relief they brought flooding and the dreaded malaria. The once bustling port city of Madras (current-day Chennai) appeared abandoned, lifeless and desolate, filled with only the stench of disease and death. It was only their faith in God that had sustained a gaunt and wasted people stricken by violent fits of fever and chills.

"My father was only seventeen then. His parents had sent him to the store to buy *vibhuti* (sacred ash), like the ash on our foreheads that honors Lord Shiva," Thatha said.

What a noise and fuss and chattering there was in the harbor area that day. The young man became distracted by the commotion. Within a few moments, from those noisy voices he would learn of a voyage that was to depart imminently, and the promise of a glorious life on the sugar plantations in South Africa.

Now imagine my great-grandfather, both hesitant and determined all at once, grappling with the choice of having a brief adventure in a faraway land, one that guaranteed a well-paying job, versus a life of ongoing hunger and starvation in Tamil Nadu. We will never know what prompted such impulsiveness—but without a word, not a hint, and bereft of the slightest suspicion of warning—he climbed aboard the departing *SS Congella*. His parents saw neither the ashes nor their son again.

Poobal let out a grave little cry of anxiety, and I sat wide-eyed and bewildered, wondering whether it was divine intervention that had set our great-grandfather on a course that would forever alter his and our lives.

I looked into Thatha's eyes and saw how painful this was for him. I could not understand my great-grandfather's hastiness. In the nightmarish picture that had since gripped my attention, I pictured his grief-stricken parents, rushing feverishly through the streets, enquiring from house to house, searching desperately for him, hoping that he was safe, whilst all that time fearing the worst.

I was amazed, too shocked to enquire any more about that particular incident.

In my mind India was some faraway land overseas. Recently, and amidst much fanfare, the Ramdaries, who owned the bus assembly factory and the airplane house, had just returned from *overseas* on the *SS Karanja*. Dad had told us that their return journey took a full three weeks. I wondered how Thatha's father managed at sea for such a long time.

"My father found the journey most difficult," Thatha said. Much of the month-long passage was spent swaying and surging at sea. "My father and the other indentured people slept on the floor under the main deck." At night, if one was at just the right spot, a star and sometimes the moon would help crack the darkness in their underworld. The monotony of their journey was broken by the barking coughs of bronchitis and the scratching brought on by the constant itch of ringworm and scabies.

Upon the ship's arrival at Port Natal, which is now known as Durban, they encountered a sandbar, the low tide making it impossible to dock. It wasn't until the next morning that they were able to disembark. Despite a difficult voyage, their spirits remained buoyed.

"Their masters called them confused cockroaches," Thatha said.

Now our situation in South Africa was beginning to make sense. Cockroaches made me understand why we were regarded as irritating outsiders, people who were not fully accepted here. So, the angry lady on the street didn't just want us to go back to Duffs Road as I had initially thought; she was demanding that we return to India. Why was she insisting on this now, more than a hundred years since Indian people had arrived here? Why hadn't my great-grandfather returned to our homeland any earlier?

Thatha's father could neither read nor write the English language. Like the other workers aboard the ship, my great-grandfather believed he was only coming for a short stay. He didn't grasp the consequences of pressing his right thumbprint onto the legal document that laid out the terms of their agreement. Unknowingly, he had agreed to a one-way journey to the sugar plantations of South Africa, binding himself to this contract for a minimum of five years. Before having any chance of returning to India, he would have to endure an additional five years in the colony as a non-indentured individual. Moreover, he would have to bear the entire cost of the return voyage. With his wage of ten shillings per month (equivalent to about twelve dollars per month in today's money, adjusted for inflation), it would have taken a lifetime's earnings to pay for the journey back home.

He was trapped in a life of indentured labor, forever confined to this place, with little hope of reuniting with his family in India.

"One hundred and fifty thousand Indians came to South Africa as laborers," Thatha continued. "They were brought here to work in the cane fields, because the British found that the local people were too lazy and unreliable."

He casually referred to the local people as lazy, presenting it as an accepted truth, and spoke with a certainty that suggested it was a widely-held belief. It was unclear how he came to hold such an opinion. Was he merely echoing what had been passed down from one generation to another, or did he genuinely believe it? At that time, I couldn't fully comprehend it. However, Thatha possessed an immense capacity for grace and compassion, which makes it hard for me to believe that he harbored any ill intentions.

The moon was high in the night sky, and, amidst the symphony of chirping crickets and croaking frogs, Thatha's story had reached its conclusion. There were so many things that I yearned to learn about my family's early experiences in South Africa. In the weeks that followed, I bombarded Thatha and Dad with questions. During this period, they recounted the many stories that were passed down from one generation to the next.

Thatha was born in 1902 in Mount Edgecombe, which was one of several sugar-milling towns that dotted the coastline to the north of Durban. People commonly referred to this place as 'the barracks.' These were bleak and cold military-style rows of crudely-plastered block buildings, with asbestos roofs and outer walls that were splotched with dull yellow paint. There were times when as many as fourteen people were squeezed into the two rooms in Thatha's home. The communal bathing facilities and bucket-system toilets had to be shared by an entire row of dwellings.

Every morning his mother would rise at three o'clock to get the open fireplace going. After cleaning her teeth with a peach twig dipped in a mixture of crushed charcoal and fine salt, she began preparing the day's meal. The sugar estate to which they were indentured provided rations of dhal, mealie-meal (cornmeal), and sugar. She grew green beans, cabbages, cauliflower, and coriander in the little garden behind their home. Some people had chicken coops, but meat was not something they had on a regular basis. Instead, the family often relied on salted dried fish. There were times when they ate stiff mealie-meal porridge and inhaled the aroma of the dried fish that hung from a string in the kitchen.

For six days a week the mill bell that rang at daybreak marked the start of my great-grandparents' workday. They grabbed a bite—caked and slightly burnt mealie-rice (maize rice) from the previous night's supper—and hurried off to the fields. They toiled from dawn until dusk, their bodies bent and strained under the relentless and oppressive African sun. My great-grandmother joined her group of women, weeding the fields and spreading manure around the young cane plants. My great-grandfather cut the mature stalks with a cane-knife (cutlass), stacked them into neat bundles, and loaded them onto the ox-driven wagons. While they worked, White men on horseback monitored their every move, wielding the whip on anyone who slackened in pace.

Come supper time, Thatha, his sister, and their father sat in a row, cross-legged, on a grass mat in the passageway that separated the living quarters from the outdoor kitchen. Thatha's mother placed a freshly cut banana leaf in front of each of them, setting an extra one for herself beside her husband. On each leaf she served a spoonful of mealie-rice, a ladle of dhal, and some vegetable curry, which could include braised sugarcane herbs, cabbage, or curried green beans.

In the innocence of my childhood I did not understand the meaning of slavery, but it was clear that a slave's lot is a cruel one. Even as a child I could feel the strain of manual labor bearing down on my great-grandfather and imagine the searing pain inflicted by the lash upon his back. Yet beyond the visceral sensations, I was struck by the anxiety and unease that is triggered by feeling trapped. How much worse it all sounded: that they did not have the means to break free from this predicament?

Our family, too, bore the weight of displacement, caught in limbo, an 'in-between' existence, belonging to neither India nor South Africa. I noticed the transformation in Thatha's demeanor whenever he spoke about his mother—an immediate shift in his tone, a loss of control over his words. It seemed as though he was struggling to contain his emotions, as if revealing them openly would somehow diminish his stoic nature.

Dad told me how his grandmother carried a profound sadness, how she struggled to adjust to her new life that was so different from the traditions of her South Indian village. Everything was unfamiliar: the landscape, the local language, the rules that were imposed upon the barracks, and even the food.

"She longed for her mother's embrace and the scent of sweet jasmine in her hair," Dad said.

All this sounded depressing, but my spirits were lifted one day when I heard Thatha say to Dad, "I can tell you with certainty that we never saw ourselves as slaves." The words flowed resolutely from his lips, almost triumphantly, and devoid of regret or bitterness. In a peculiar way, our family's entrapment and harsh existence liberated them into a cynical kind of freedom. Now that they were stuck in South Africa, class, caste, and religion mattered much less. They had to pull together and shape their lives around community and connection.

"My father made a *bowlah*," Thatha recounted. He explained how his father transformed a six-gallon paraffin container by carving slats into the sides to allow for ventilation. He filled the bottom with wood chips and coal, remnants that had fallen from the steam locomotives. On frosty winter nights the *bowlah* would come to life, drawing neighbors around its warm glow. People shared tales from their motherland, raised their voices to the strains of traditional songs, and reminisced about the cherished memories of the villages of their childhood.

Among the numerous maxims that Thatha embraced, there was one that held resonance: "The beauty of education lies in its permanence; it can never be taken away." Education held a place of utmost importance in the lives of indentured people. For Thatha, education was second only to God. Over time, the community united to establish their own schools, offering instruction in both English and Tamil. These institutions became pillars for preserving the rich cultural heritage of South India, nurturing artistic expressions through music, dance, and theatrical traditions.

When Thatha turned twenty, his father insisted that he marry. The concept of arranged love felt harsh and dreadful to him. In a strange twist of fate, Thatha ended up marrying his sister's daughter, a girl six years his junior. After the untimely passing of his parents, Thatha shouldered the responsibility of providing for his extended family. He worked as a carpenter and later as a bricklayer at Natal Estates. The three thick horizontal stripes of ash on his forehead served as a testament to his unwavering faith in the Hindu deity Shiva. It was this faith that instilled in him a profound sense of spiritual belonging.

"Everything is connected, and we are connected to everything," he would often say. "Though our roots may lie in India, and we will always hold an emotional attachment to our motherland, this is our home now, and this is where we truly belong."

CHAPTER 4

The Roots of My Ambition

It was a year later, sometime in December of 1967, and three months since the birth of my sister, Devi. All signs of my mother's recent pregnancy had subsided, and she was busy cleaning sheep's head and trotters in our back yard. *Ama* was the Tamil name by which we addressed my mother.

A large pot of water bubbled over flaming logs in the fire pit. Ama sat on her haunches, her sari loosely ruffled around her and her cheeks glistening a pearly rosé. There was soot on the tip of her nose and a fire of determination in her eye as she stoked the flames with her breath. Anyone who observed Ama in that moment would not have realized that she had been crowned Carnival Queen in middle school.

"Don't stand too close. The smoke will get in your eyes," she said. Sweat dripped off her forehead, and a smoky glaze filled her eyes.

Ama reached into the fire and carefully retrieved a footlong strip of flaming iron. Clutching the end wrapped in a strip of cloth, she meticulously worked the contours of the sheep's head and feet. Every bit of hair was singed, leaving the skin scorched and leathery. With a charred odor hanging in the air, she put on a grand display of surgical precision. The sheep's eyes were scalloped out of their sockets, the tongue severed from its base, the hooves disarticulated, and the skull expertly cleaved down the center.

"Speed and accuracy, that's what you need to succeed at school, Krish." It was customary for us to have two names: a home name, and a school name taken from our birth certificate. My close friends and family called me Krish, after the flute-playing god who is often depicted as a cowherd surrounded by a bevy of beautiful women.

Ama switched modes, delicately scooping up the brain into her cupped hands and delivering it into a bowl. She raised her head and looked at me intently. "You are a smart boy," she said. "Your great-grandfather worked in the sugarcane fields, your grandfather is a carpenter, and Dad is a clerk in an underwear company. You can be anything you wish to be, but I think you should be a doctor, Krish."

Was it pride? Conceit? I could not tell, but a warm, satisfied feeling rose inside of me. I absorbed her words silently, caught up in my mother's ambitions, her delight in my potential, and her dreams for me to be a doctor. Just hearing her say this made it feel like it had already happened, and as though I didn't have to do anything more.

Ama was the third of ten sisters. The elusive boy arrived at number eleven, and her parents could finally stop. We would jest that her siblings alone could have formed a cricket team. Ama bore a striking resemblance to her maternal grandmother, who hailed from the horse-owning Khan lineage in Pathankot, in northern India. She possessed a fairer complexion and taller stature than her sisters. In later years some people mockingly called her Snow-White Aunty. She had no need for the skin-lightening facial cream that was popular at the time.

Ama was an ambitious woman and she saw in all her children the vehicle by which her dreams could be realized. She was fully aware of the sacrifices required to succeed and was resolute in ensuring our triumph. As the eldest I bore the weight of those dreams. In exchange, I received certain privileges, especially at mealtimes. Whenever we could afford it, Ama would offer me the choicest pieces of lean mutton, and allow me to remove the fatty skin from the chicken and enjoy the pure white meat along the breastbone. Perhaps more importantly, I could steer away from tripe, sheep's head curry, and sheep's lungs, which she politely glossed as 'soft liver.'

As Ama set the table for dinner that evening, it was evident that she was in no mood to compromise.

"Krish, why don't you give the trotters a try? Just a taste? You won't know if you like it until you try."

"I prefer plain sugar beans and *roti*. Why spoil it with trotters?"

While the rest of the family was engrossed in stripping the meat off the sheep's feet, Poobal took pleasure in taunting me by noisily slurping the slippery marrow. Down to the last grain of rice and the final sliver of cartilage, their bowls were soon empty. I, on the other hand, was left fiddling around, picking out the beans from the curry, and fussing over what was onion and what was marrow.

After dinner Thatha and Dad were engaged in a deep conversation, captivated by an event that was splashed all over the newspapers and broadcast on every radio station. The *Daily News* reported:

> "Dr. Christiaan Barnard performed the world's first human heart transplant operation on 3 December 1967. The operation, which lasted nine hours and used a team of thirty people, was performed at Cape Town's Groote Schuur Hospital."

Despite my attempts to listen to their discussion, my frustration from dinner proved too much of a distraction. Ama must have noticed my curiosity as her demeanor had softened considerably.

"Would you like some scrambled eggs instead?" she asked.

Though my palate was contaminated with the flavor of trotters, I finished the eggs and felt a whole lot better. It is strange how easily an unshackled mind can free the tongue. Little did I know that cooked sheep's brain can be cleverly disguised to resemble scrambled eggs.

That night as I drifted off to sleep, my mind was filled with wonder about the heart transplant. Though I did not understand the details, I found the idea of putting spare parts into the human body quite fascinating. How could they take a heart that had stopped beating in one person and put it into another? And how did they manage to get it started again?

The next morning, I found Dad dressed for work, sitting at the kitchen table with the *Daily News* spread out before him. He wore his usual faraway look, gazing out of the window and absently stirring a grain of salt into his black coffee.

"All it takes is a grain of salt to bring out the sweetness in coffee," Dad often said.

I knew he was still in awe of the heart transplant, replaying the complex drama in his head. But I also knew that he saw no ambition in it. Unlike Ama, he was content to live his life within the confines of his routine, even if it meant missing out on the excitement of the extraordinary.

Dad, the eldest of four children, was born in the barracks at Mount Edgecombe. He completed his grade twelve at an English school and finished grade eight in his Tamil education. Observing him at the kitchen table—in his crisp brown English suit and matching tie, a Parker pen prominently displayed in his breast pocket, and the three thick stripes of ashes on his forehead—one would not have guessed that he was as carefree and innocent as a yellow rubber duck floating on a vast ocean. He was content to rise and fall with the tide, and even twirl in the eddies at times.

Dad said goodbye to each of us, patting Poobal's head, ruffling my hair, and giving Ama a peck on her cheek. As he made his way towards the front door, his sister rushed over and attempted to wipe the ashes from his forehead. She was embarrassed that he displayed his faith in such a public manner. Dad, refusing to be swayed, gently held back his sister's hand and kissed her on the forehead.

With Dad now gone for the day, Poobal and I quickly finished our tea and Marie biscuits so that we could set about exploring the vast possibilities outside.

Our backyard was a veritable orchard, with two of every kind of fruit tree: peaches, guavas, avocados, bananas, mulberries, and pawpaws (papaya). Thatha had thoughtfully ensured that Poobal and I would never squabble over such matters. But that didn't stop us from bragging about whose guavas were bigger, which mangoes tasted better, or whose avocado trees yielded more fruit.

Thatha encouraged us to wander freely, to invent and experiment, without worrying about any consequences. He also allowed us unrestricted access to his tool collection, stored in dusty wooden boxes in the cobweb-filled cellar under our house. We had everything we needed: hammers, chisels, vintage manual hand drills, hacksaws, and nails and screws of every size and shape. But that day, we had something different in mind, something more creative than carrying out unwarranted repairs on our relatives' furniture. Together with our next-door neighbors, we were going to embark on a musical adventure.

I picked up the hacksaw and headed toward *my* pawpaw tree. With care, I cut off a long branch, making sure to keep the leaves at the end intact. Then I shaped a beveled mouthpiece on the cut edge and carved several holes of varying sizes along the stem. The final result was a cross between a trumpet and a flute. Meanwhile, Poobal stretched out the inner rubber tube of a tire over an old plastic bucket, creating his own version of a drum.

The aunty from next door had already begun washing her clothes, and soon her children, Anil, Kamal, and Vishnu, would join us. Anil was one year my senior, while Kamal and Vishnu were one year apart from Poobal. We could hear Anil tuning the chords on his makeshift banjo, tightening screws and adjusting the fishing-gut strings.

Ama brought out our laundry and wrapped a plastic apron around her sari. She set the bundle down, put her hands on her hips, and cast me a threatening glance. I knew she was upset because I was wearing "visiting clothes." By the end of the day, the white safari suit would be a completely unrecognizable mess, stained with dirt mixed in with leafy-green chlorophyll streaks.

Washday provided a perfect opportunity for the daughters-in-law from the two households to engage in communal venting about life's troubles. In between soaking, lathering, and rinsing, they usually discussed topics that were filled with sudsy gossip. On that particular morning, the usual tattle was put on hold as everyone spoke of nothing else but the recent heart transplant.

It was unusual, but instead of using their names, the two ladies addressed each other as "sister-in-law."

"What a thing, sister-in-law, to actually take a beating heart from a young girl and put it into an older man," said the aunty from next door.

Ama shuddered at the thought. "And to think that it's still beating, sister-in-law. I don't think I could handle someone else's heart inside me."

"But think of it as a blessing, sister-in-law," the aunty continued. "The memory of the dead person can live on through another."

Ama shook her head. "I'm still scared by the idea of my blood mixing with a part of someone else's body. I worry that it would change me, and I would become a different person altogether."

By now, our friends from next door had joined us and our barefoot marching band had picked up the tempo. The squeaky twang of a banjo, the high-pitched squealing of the paw-paw-stem trumpet, and the boom of drums filled the air. Despite the clamor, our moms pretended not to notice our little troupe advancing. The cacophony of sounds came to a sudden halt, and we found ourselves directly in between where our mothers stood.

All the talk about the heart transplant had sparked a desire in me to become a doctor. I had dressed up that day out of curiosity, but at that moment the idea presented itself more vividly and with greater conviction.

"I am going to be a doctor too!" I proclaimed without any hint of hesitation.

My uttering those words surprised me almost as much as it did the others. Having committed myself with such daring, what more could I do than wait and see the sort of response it would elicit.

Anil's mother looked up from her washing, surveyed me from head to toe, and put on a knowing expression.

"You want to be a doctor too?" she said. Then she turned confidently towards Ama and spoke in a serious and exalted manner. "Sister-in-law, I know he's going to be a doctor. Look, he's even dressed like a doctor."

Several months following the ground-breaking heart transplant, and, with grade one still a full year away, Ama placed my clothes onto a bedsheet gathered the ends, and knotted them. I lifted the bundle and set off to the preschool that my maternal grandmother ran at her home in Redhill.

The village of Redhill was five or six kilometers away from Duffs Road and took its name from the loose red sand which covered that area. My grandparents rented a small wood and iron house that was nestled in between a banana plantation and a mango grove. They cooked on a wood-fired stove and relied on kerosene lamps for lighting. My mother's sisters, and there were many, ironed their clothes with a thick triangular slab of cast-iron that they heated on the stove.

The day before I started at the preschool, a travelling barber arrived on his bicycle. He carefully cleaned off his equipment with methylated spirits. After placing a shallow plastic bowl over the top of my head, he used his number-one hand clipper to shear off all the hair that stuck out below. Then he thinned out and shaped what was left.

"The dish cut will help you focus," said Redhill Ayah.

Neil Armstrong had not yet walked on the moon, and the dish cut was a fashion statement driven by misaligned extremes. People compared it either to the short-cropped hair of earlier astronauts, or to the inmates of reform schools that delivered cold showers at five in the morning. At the time, when the hippie movement was celebrated and long hair was in fashion, I felt a strong sense of irritation, and could not help but identify with the reformatory look.

The memory of that first day of preschool remains clear in my mind. I recall the crisp sound of the brass bell that Ayah rang to signal the beginning of class, and her standing out front in her white sari with her hair coiled into a tight bun, and a rhinestone nose-ring sparkling in the morning light.

There were perhaps fifteen of us in all, eager preschoolers who took our places on a few wooden benches that were plonked in the red sand. Redhill Ayah painstakingly etched each letter of the alphabet onto her slate, and with each stroke, the sound of her soapstone pencil scraping against the surface reverberated in my mind. Sometimes we copied the letters onto our own slates. However, what I remember was Redhill Ayah taking my index finger and coursing it through the red sand. Even with my eyes closed, I could easily recreate the shape of each symbol in my mind. At night, as I lay in bed trying to fall asleep, the fingers of my imagination would instinctively trace the curves and strokes of the alphabet.

While juggling the task of preventing the dhal from boiling over, shuffling rice in a woven cane *muram* (winnower), and tossing the chaff into the sunlight, Ayah also taught us the basics of the alphabet, and counting from one to ten. With her guidance I quickly progressed to phonetically sounding out words. Redhill Ayah was taken aback when I read out my first word.

"Spar-let-ta," I said, pointing to the name of a soft drink that was printed in bold letters on a brown paper grocery bag.

After several months at Ayah's preschool, it was time for me to return to Duffs Road.

The day I declared my ambition to become a doctor marked the beginning of a newfound earnestness in my pursuit of knowledge. I developed a voracious appetite for learning and whenever I encountered a new word or concept that I didn't understand, I was relentless in unloading a barrage of questions upon Dad:

"When you were a kid, were the stars still in the sky, Dad?" I would ask.

"Yes, son, they have always been there."

"Where do the stars go during the day?

Dad smiled, "They are always in the sky, son. We can only see them when it gets dark at night."

"Why are stars so sparkly and shiny?"

"Some stars give off more light than others"

"Can stars fall from the sky, Dad?"

"All right, slow down there, son. How about we take a break and save some questions for tomorrow?"

To me, it seemed like Dad knew everything; he could recall people's names, important dates, and even the most obscure places in the world. We enjoyed playing the "Capital City" game, and though I had never heard of Mali before, I quickly learned that its capital city was Timbuktu—I liked the sound of that: Timbuktu, it stuck.

Ama also played her part in nurturing my curiosity. She found delight in the most obscure collective nouns. For those that were unknown to her, she consulted *The Students' Companion*, by Wilfred D. Best. Sometimes we would try to catch Dad out, but he had no problem, even with the difficult ones, like 'a murder of crows.' If I recall correctly, only 'a tower of giraffes' stumped him.

When we appeared to be running out of questions, Ama introduced me to a quiz show that was on Springbok Radio at 10 p.m. on Friday nights—*Venture,* hosted by Kim Shippey. After supper we listened to *The Mind of Tracey Dark*, where Tracy demonstrated her psychic abilities by bending spoons and moving objects with her mind. This was followed by the crime series *Squad Cars*. Dad would leave shortly thereafter to play Brag with his friends. That's what he did every Friday night. I struggled to stay awake until 10 p.m., but Ama always found ways to rekindle my waning enthusiasm so that I could make it to the start of *Venture*.

"Think how impressed Anil will be when you tell him that Herodotus is the father of history," she once told me.

"Who cares about that, Ma," I would counter.

"Write it down. Write the question and the answer next to it, so you won't forget, Krish."

The details that I memorized were a mixed bag of quirky and often useless information, but it worked like catnip on my brain, making me curious and training my mind to remember facts.

As my quest for knowledge grew, so did my desire to succeed. Losing at Checkers or Snakes and Ladders would often make me cry, regardless of whether my opponent was an adult or not. I hated to lose, but nothing upset me more than winning when I knew that Dad had deliberately thrown a game.

"Last game, Krish, it's already 11 o' clock," he would say. And when that game was over, I would complain.

"You let me win because you want to go to bed," I would say. "We must play another game, and this time, you must teach me about that special move you made."

We would only stop playing when I felt I had beaten him fairly, or I went to bed in tears.

With six months to go before the start of grade one, I began to create a window into the universe that I perceived to be medicine. I had no idea what it would take to become a doctor but I was determined to get a head start. One can't go wrong with the parts of the human body, I thought. That was a good place to begin. I dutifully covered an unlined notebook with the brown paper from the Sparletta bag and labelled the front with my name. The paper, though a bit thick, would at least match the way children in primary school covered and labelled their textbooks.

When I think of that time, I see myself at the table that Thatha had made, working outside in the front verandah, under the light of a hot gooseneck lamp, and with easels flying about in the summer night. After Dad was done with the *Daily News*, I would carefully clip out the anatomical drawings from the health section. Each week, there were sketch drawings of the heart, the eye, the brain, and several other organs. I trimmed the pictures and, using a paste made from flour and water, placed them neatly into the notebook. All of this had to be studied, copied out, and absorbed. I threw myself into every little detail, memorizing iris, ventricles, and aorta, and painstakingly tracing out crude sketches of the heart onto small pieces of paper.

While Poobal and Vishnu ran about with water-pistols, playing cops and robbers, and Anil identified with great precision every make of car that passed by, I was perfecting my surgical skills on unsuspecting subjects that happened to cross my path. The yellow-jacketed grasshoppers—that I used to practice chip shots on, with the Bobby Locke eight iron that Thatha's boss had given him—became the first specimens for my dissection. However, the offensive smell of their squishy insides quickly forced me to abandon them. The crabs from the stream at the bottom end of our garden presented a more interesting challenge. Once I had got hold of their pincers, I could easily turn them onto their backs, open their bellies, and unleash the tiny little baby crabs into the world.

The Christmas before my grade one year, in December of 1968, I received a plastic doctor set from my parents. Thatha and Ayah pretended to play patients, and I listened to their hearts, peeped into their ears, and administered fake injections.

On the week leading up to the start of school, I approached Anil to ask if he knew who the father of history was. Anil was not pleased with being shown up in such a manner. "You fucking bastard, wait till Black Botie catches you at school," he shouted.

CHAPTER 5

Lost in Translation

Ama swore by *The Students' Companion*. That book alone held the might of transforming a mediocre English student into an excellent one. Each night when supper was done, I sat at the kitchen table and studied the book, memorizing endless rows of smart words, similes, and idioms. Later, I would march up and down the house, with *The Students' Companion* in hand, and launch into a perfect shower of sparkling phrases.

A few days after Anil had called me a fucking bastard, and at great risk of inviting another torrent of expletives, I was once again peppering him with a sentence constructed with random words from *The Students' Companion*.

"Don't perambulate around the outskirts of verbosity," I told him.

"Wow, you know such big words, Krish," he replied.

I was thankful that he never enquired as to the meaning of that sentence, because I had no idea what those words meant.

Unless we knew English and knew it well, all doors were closed to us. It was the language of power and the ticket to a university education in our province, one of the last strongholds of English influence in South Africa.

Though the prevailing language in our house was English, my grandparents conversed with each other in our mother tongue, Tamil. These linguistic differences gradually seeped into our daily interactions and occasionally took on an air of casual animosity. Poobal and I often delighted in laying ideological traps for our grandparents.

I remember the time when Poobal held up some carrots we had plucked from the garden, and with mischief twinkling in his eyes, inquired, "Is this a fruit, Thatha?"

"It's a vejje-table," Thatha replied.

"You're so silly, Thatha," I chimed in. "It's not vejje-table, it's a vegetable."

Thatha would playfully reprimand us, using the Tamil words *thunsil kooties*, which meant naughty children. Whenever our grandparents spoke Tamil, we thought of them as being backwards and out of touch with the times.

On the night before my first day of grade one, in January of 1969, I lay in bed while Ama ironed my school shirt. She was almost six months into her fourth pregnancy then. My sister Thiliga was due in May. I watched as she worked the tip of the iron into the wrinkled creases, the smell of the wet heat permeating the air.

Ama placed the iron back onto its cradle, fixing her gaze on me. Her eyes lit up, and a warm smile spread across her face. "Tomorrow is a big day, Krish," she said. Then she narrowed her eyes and furrowed her brow, "You need to get up early, so it's time to sleep now."

Before switching off the lights she carefully folded my white shirt and laid it beside the rest of my school uniform: a navy-blue pair of pants, black socks, tie, and blazer with the school's official monogram.

That night as I lay in bed, I tossed and turned in the darkness, haunted by Anil's warning about Black Botie. I was afraid that I would end up in her class.

Black Botie also lived in Duffs Road. One day I watched through the window as she and Ayah were talking outside. After she left, I approached Ayah and inquired if that person was indeed Black Botie. Aya was a kind-hearted soul, and she was deeply disturbed, offended that I had referred to the lady as being black; not only did that derogatory name imply that she was black, but that she was so black that even her entrails (*botie*) were stained black. Later, my father cautioned me never to speak about people in such a manner.

"You will call her Mrs. Pillay," he said. I could not get the name Black Botie out of my mind. It stuck.

Anil claimed that Black Botie was "a cruel teacher." Once he told me about an encounter he had with her. He gave a seemingly honest account. However, I wondered whether she really was the terror he had made her out to be.

Even in casual conversations, Anil appeared to believe that swear words were an ordinary part of the English language. This habit spilled over into the school environment. One day, when he uttered the F-word, Black Botie approached him. Without saying anything, she seized him by the earlobe and deposited him into the large garbage bin tucked away in the corner of the classroom.

"You'll sit in the dirt until you clean up your language," she declared.

"Then she applied Sunlight soap to my tongue and instructed me to rinse out my mouth," Anil recounted.

As I drifted off to sleep, I pictured myself standing beside my desk with outstretched palms and an entire class trembling with fear. Black Botie was striding up and down the rows, ruler in hand, and calling out random math problems. I could sense the sting of the ruler on my palm as I stumbled over a simple sum: "two plus seven."

When I awoke at dawn, on my first day of primary school, I noticed that Thatha had already departed for work. On the table beside our bed I discovered a stack of bronze coins: one cent for each way of the five-kilometer bus journey to and from school, along with three cents of spending money.

After breakfast, Dad helped me knot my tie. I ran the comb through my hair, attempting to style it in a manner reminiscent of John Lennon's—dry, straight, with a mop-like appearance on top. Ama would have none of that. Despite my objections, she drenched my hair in coconut oil and coifed it to a wispy perfection. As if that weren't enough, she hugged me and kissed me on the lips. I rushed out of the door, making frantic attempts to remove any traces of lipstick.

The bus stop stood below the bus assembly factory, in the perilous 'arc of death,' a treacherous bend that was the site of numerous accidents. I joined the other newbies, and we eagerly lined up like energetic, unbridled ponies, jockeying for position, vying to be first on board. The PUTCO bus came chugging and grinding around the corner, swaying erratically like a drunken donkey before jerking to a halt. I climbed the steep stairs and placed my one cent on the metal tray. It settled with a clang. The bus-driver, an African man, scowled as he handed me my ticket, leaving me bewildered as to why he was so angry.

The Kasturba Gandhi Primary School stood proudly on a terraced hill in the Phoenix Settlement that was situated 15 kilometers (about 9.32 miles) north of central Durban. The school was built by Mahatma Gandhi in 1954 and bore the name of his wife, Kasturba. The school—which received funding from both the state and the Phoenix Settlement Trust established by Gandhi—followed apartheid regulations and enrolled only Indian students.

The school's Romanesque podium, from where the principal recited the Lord's Prayer each morning, stood out in stark contrast to the surroundings: ten worn-out classrooms, dusty grounds, shattered windows, and mosquito-filled water tanks. In the foreground, lush green meadows gently sloped towards a babbling stream. There were better-equipped schools closer to our home, but my parents took great pride in sending me in the opposite direction, to Gandhi's School.

After the morning assembly I waited anxiously in room one, anticipating the arrival of our form teacher. Much to my relief, Black Botie was not the one who came through the door that morning.

After the first two years of primary school, the beads of the abacus and the linseed smell of modeling plasticine gave way to poetry, prose, and punctuation, the requisite skills for perfecting English.

During our English lessons our teachers had us memorize and recite poems by renowned English poets. Our weekly assignments included William Wordsworth's *Daffodils*, Alfred Lord Tennyson's *The Brook*, and Samuel Taylor Coleridge's *The Rime of the Ancient Mariner*. *The Brook* held a special place in my heart because it was a poem that Ama had also studied during her time in school. Together we would playfully recite the opening lines, "I come from haunts of coot and hern, I make a sudden sally/And sparkle out among the fern/To bicker down a valley…"

School was a realm where poetry was paramount. As we mechanically recited lines from memory, our teacher observed us with the zeal of a hog hunting for truffles, poised to seize upon any missed words or faltering delivery. Errors were met with a disdainful snort, incomprehensible muttering, and the sting of a narrow ruler striking down upon the fingertips of the transgressor. I was a curious boy, but our educational institutions showed little regard for nurturing inventiveness; their mission focused on suppressing creative thinking and ensuring strict adherence to rote learning. Succeeding in primary school followed a simple dictum: memorize, memorize, memorize.

In the beginning of my grade three year, a petite young lady in a red sleeveless dress entered our classroom. She carried a stack of neatly rolled-up charts that were secured with a rubber band. She placed the charts on the table, gave a faint sigh, and proceeded to the window. Without uttering a word, she picked up a roll from the table and held it up to the light, peering through it like a pirate scanning the horizon. A frog sprang forth from inside the rolled chart and emitted a loud and solitary croak. The lady let out a shriek, leapt backwards, and found herself perched upon the table with her legs tucked beneath her. The entire class erupted in uncontrollable laughter.

The introduction of our Afrikaans teacher, Mrs. Soobramoney, was certainly memorable. While her encounter with a frog had us in stitches, Mrs. Soobramoney demanded strict discipline in the classroom. She was a consummate professional and tried her best to make Afrikaans lessons more engaging. She introduced us to comic books and encouraged role-play.

Studying Afrikaans as a second language was obligatory for us. When I think about Afrikaans, I am reminded of the traditional wedding recipe inspired by an Old English rhyme: 'Something old, something new, something borrowed, something blue, and a sixpence in your shoe.' In the mid-1800s, Afrikaans emerged as a new creole language with its roots in Old Dutch. It assimilated words from Khoekhoe and San, Malay, Indonesian, and Portuguese. However, the Afrikaner nation disregarded its diverse origins and marginalized the linguistic heritage of other speakers. They referred to the language as 'Burgher' Afrikaans, and elevated it to the status of a pure Germanic language, using it as a symbol of their cultural distinctiveness.

While my classmates found enjoyment in our Afrikaans lessons, I couldn't connect with the subject. It seemed as if I had developed a natural aversion towards it. Perhaps this reluctance was intertwined with the anxiety I felt towards English. I often wondered, "What value does Afrikaans hold, aside from hindering my progress in English?" It was unfortunate, but I projected this negative attitude onto the Indian teachers who taught Afrikaans. Their wholehearted embrace of something so foreign perplexed me, and I struggled to understand their enthusiasm and sincerity in the way they taught the language.

The pervasive influence of English culture, the allure of new and modern ideas, and the perceived superiority of the Queen's English were gradually setting me adrift from my Indian heritage. I was becoming more English and less Indian, sailing away from a past that seemed less relevant, and towards a future that promised greater possibilities. I rejected traditional Indian clothing, favored English music, and even though I knew it was frowned upon by Hindus, I found myself irresistibly drawn to Eskort pork sausages. And after we prayed, I would quickly wipe the three stripes of ash off my forehead, feeling ashamed of displaying my faith in public.

Thatha steadfastly believed that invoking the blessings of Mother Saraswathi, the goddess of education, was the key to acquiring a good education.

"Only then will your mind be clear to absorb what you are being taught at school," he would say.

Following the Saraswathi *puja* in my grade three year—during which we reverently presented milk and fruits before an altar adorned with a framed picture of Mother Saraswathi and a brass statue of Lord Ganesha—Thatha decided that the rudimentary fragments of 'kitchen Tamil' that we had gleaned from our grandparents were no longer sufficient. Amidst the lingering fragrance of burning incense sticks, and with our math and science textbooks thoughtfully positioned to receive divine blessings, Thatha resolved that Poobal and I should learn Tamil.

We started our Tamil lessons soon after we began learning Afrikaans at school. Every evening, after washing our hands and feet, Poobal and I joined Thatha on the front verandah, and together, we offered a Tamil prayer of gratitude to the goddess Saraswathi. Thatha began our lesson like a maestro conducting his orchestra—by raising a green stick he had crafted from the branch of a peach tree.

One evening in early 1971, approximately three months into our Tamil lessons, Thatha proudly presented a painstakingly-crafted chart that he'd made with a borrowed felt-tipped pen. It was a remarkable display of calligraphy that included the letters of the Tamil alphabet.

The lesson began with a recap of what had been learned so far.

"*Aana, avina, eenaa,*" said Thatha.

Poobal and I repeated, "Anna, avina, eenaa."

"Not Anna. Stretch out the 'aaa' sound. Say *aana*," Thatha corrected us.

We replied, "Aaaana."

Then Thatha informed us that there are thirty-one letters in the Tamil alphabet, twelve vowels and eighteen consonants.

"That's only thirty, Thatha," I said, mocking his inability to count.

"So, you think you're too clever! I was not finished. Tamil has one character that is neither a vowel nor a consonant. Thirty-one letters. See?"

Now it was my ego that was bruised, and I could not handle it.

"This is too difficult. How many languages do we have to learn?" I stormed out of the lesson and ran towards Ama.

That night at the dinner table there was an atmosphere of siege, a foreboding that something was to be sacrificed. I could see it in Thatha's eyes, in Ama's disapproving frown, and in Dad's furrowed brow.

"English is the future, *Naina* (Father)," Dad began hesitantly, lowering his head to avoid direct eye contact with Thatha.

Thatha appeared detached at first, but when he spoke it was measured, melodic, and with words that had the intensity to appeal to the heavens.

"Everything in our world, every grain of sand, every ray of light, the plants, the animals, the sun, the stars, all have a voice. Our language sounds so sweet, like music. Tamil holds everything together for us: our culture, our traditions, our religion. Our language makes us who we are."

He paused momentarily and began again suddenly, with defiance leaping up in him as though he were thirty or forty years younger. Color rushed into his exhausted face, there was a gleam of fire in his lusterless eyes, and Thatha's voice trembled. The words that came from his lips, that had clearly been prepared and thought out long ago, were now hurrying along, unrestrained, and like a stone hurtling down a hill of resentment.

"The British tried to break us," he said. "When our hands and feet cracked and were bleeding from working in the cane-fields, our Tamil songs kept us going. When my father was weak from hunger—when we only had a drink of sour porridge and smelt the dry fish because there was no money for meat—our Tamil stories gave us courage to go to work the next day."

He spoke passionately of the British attempts to crush their spirit, likening their treatment to that of slaves. In the depths of their despair, the Tamil language became a source of light and hope, guiding them through the darkest of times. Despite the British efforts to deny them education, Tamil schools emerged as beacons of knowledge, liberating them from the chains of ignorance.

Ama had finished the dishes. She wiped her wet hands on her apron before sitting at the kitchen table. Thatha turned to her, his face radiant with sincerity and his voice filled with a profound spiritual beauty.

"Remember the Arundhati Star?" he asked, referring to the stars that my parents had both pointed to on their wedding night. (The binary star system, located in the Bear constellation, featured two stars revolving around each other, in contrast to most star pairs where only one star rotated while the other remained stationary.) Thatha reminded my parents of our culture's belief in the equality of men and women. The traditional practice of pointing to that particular star complex on their wedding night was a principle upheld and nurtured by our Tamil language.

The grandfather clock chimed once, on the half hour. Ama raised her gaze from the floor and clasped her hands in prayer. "*Satyam*," she responded, meaning 'truth,' believing it to be divine confirmation when the spoken word coincided exactly with the chime of the clock.

Dad was clearly torn between preserving our mother-tongue and preparing us for the future. He shuttled between English and Tamil, hoping to find the right words, some well-sounding idea that when brought out at the proper moment would soothe Thatha's feelings.

"But times have changed, *Naina*. How will they succeed at university? They're just starting to learn Afrikaans. How will they cope with three languages?"

Thatha's cheeks sank, and tears gathered in his eyes. His voice carried the weight of exhaustion and the pain of one defeated.

"They want to erase our culture, our identity, and our language," he said. "They make us feel ashamed of who we are and want us to forget our history. They teach their ways and their culture so that, in the end, we don't know who we truly are. People who don't know their identity wander around the earth like useless puppets."

"It's the law, *Naina*. Only English and Afrikaans are taught at school. I wish the children could learn Tamil in school, but it's not permitted. I understand that they don't teach the history of our people, but what can we do?"

That night I lay awake, resisting the temptation to hold onto Thatha's earlobe, a peculiar habit that I used to ease my way to sleep. The discussion that evening was profoundly confusing. I cannot articulate with certainty the emotions I felt. What I recall is an immense feeling of guilt, burdened by the responsibility for causing such turmoil. Above all else, I couldn't forgive myself for making Thatha so sad. I wished for some form of physical punishment, to release the tears that had welled up in me, to pretend that they were the result of pain rather than guilt. Yet what I would learn that night was that the sting of compassion hurt much more than any pain of retribution.

Thatha took hold of my hand and gently guided it to his ear.

CHAPTER 6

A Whitewashed Education

When I was in grade six, a young African boy invited me to glide along the stream that ran next to our school. It was unthinkable to venture outside the school boundaries. I could not swim and knew well the consequences if I were to be caught. Yet it was an opportunity that I could not resist. Though it was nothing like the grand Mississippi, I embraced the spirit of Jim and Huckleberry Finn. We drifted along on a raft fashioned from the upturned roof of a rusty old car, my teenage friend propelling us with a long pole. Then, one day, I heard a rustling behind the tall reeds that lined the stream and realized that my mischief had been discovered.

I found myself coming up with excuses, but the school prefect shook his head and waved me towards the principal's office. The principal, a cheerless old man, saw no adventure in my actions and rendered a swift judgment. He raised his cane and readied himself.

"Bend over and touch your toes," he said, as he unleashed 'six of the best' onto my buttocks.

Like the restrictions placed on my physical boundaries, my education was also being carefully curated, so that I might take my place in the middle ground of our racially-divided society. The practice of rote learning became entrenched, and with my mother tongue denied, English and Afrikaans were the only languages that I was exposed to.

I was in the platoon class in grade six, and our morning lessons were held in the open air. We sat on wooden benches that were arranged in orderly rows beneath the towering canopy of a giant acacia tree. In the dreamy, hazy period before lunch—when my mind wandered like a drifting cloud, lulled by the graceful movements of Wordsworth's daffodils—we were presented with lectures on the history of our country. In that illusionary state, the truth of what was conveyed was beyond question, the written text a representation of reality, and its conclusions undeniable.

A substantial portion of our textbooks was dedicated to the 'Great Trek', a pivotal event in our country's history. It documented the migration of Afrikaner farmers, who ventured northward and eastward to escape British domination. During one of our history lessons Mr. Bramdeo, our teacher, recounted a significant incident that occurred in February of 1838, just a short two-hour drive northwards from our school.

Mr. Bramdeo was a portly old gentleman who tried to impose his authority by peering sternly over his dark-rimmed glasses. His lessons often sounded as though he was broadcasting with tape-recorded precision.

"Dingaan was a wily Zulu king," said Mr. Bramdeo. "To conquer the sorcerers, he must first embody the cunning of a fox and later the strength of a lion."

Then Mr. Bramdeo paused momentarily, as though he were turning over the tape to its more glamorous Side A.

"The valiant Piet Retief led his band of intrepid Trekkers on horseback. They galloped joyously around uMgungundlovu, reveling in their epic triumph over Chief Sekonyela and the Batlôkwa tribe.

Armed with formidable guns, the Trekkers struck fear into the heart of Dingane, who had mistaken their horses for hornless cattle."

We burst into uncontrollable laughter, amused that Dingane was so stupid that he could not tell the difference between a horse and a cow.

Mr. Bramdeo paused once more, taking the opportunity to ponder, to ensure that he was going to enunciate the playback just as it was recorded.

"Dingane said to Piet Retief, 'You get cattle back from Batlôkwa, give you land from Thukela to Umzimvubu.'"

That was a vast expanse of land, the size of modern-day Portugal, that spanned the area between the Tugela and Umzimvubu rivers.

After Retief's party had successfully recovered the cattle, Dingaan invited them to his *kraal* (village). There was to be a celebration, complete with dancing and traditional Zulu beer. Dingane, after having concealed three thousand warriors on the grounds, duped Piet Retief's group into leaving their weapons outside.

Our teacher's eyes flashed with a sinister light and his face darkened into a scowl of disgust. Then his tone became deep and indifferent. He wagged his index finger sternly, exclaiming, "*Bulala umtagati! Bulala umtagati!*" which translated from Zulu means, "Kill the wizards! Kill the wizards!"

We fixed our teacher with an astonished gaze. He, on returning to his former calm, proceeded to shock us even further.

"The warriors descended upon the unsuspecting Boers and bashed in their skulls with *knobkerries* (clubs with a knob at one end). They ripped out Piet Retief's heart and liver and presented them to Dingane. The Zulu king proceeded to eat the offerings so that he might possess the same courage and bravery as the Trek leader."

For many years thereafter we would wag our fingers at one another and repeat with mischievous melody, *Bulala umtagati, bulala umtagati*. The grotesque meaning of those words, as raw and undistilled as they were, was not something that I gave much thought to. At the time, that phrase was just a phrase, catchy, amusing, and seemingly harmless.

Arresting examples of human behavior were clipped from segments of our history, stripped of any depth or complexity, and furnished in an easily-digestible lesson that would seduce us to the idea that White people were superior, and that Black people were inferior. We were also being conditioned to align with a sinister belief that African tribes were godless savages, murderous cattle thieves, and obstacles in the righteous path of the Trekkers through southern Africa.

I was still too young to register the bias of what was communicated to us, or to know about censorship and the crudeness of the devices it employed. I was also at an age when none of this alarmed me. With time, I too bought into the idea that I should be grateful for being pulled into the civilized world. How fortunate I was to be spared a life of ignorance, I thought. So giddily gracious was my acceptance of the plight and virtuosity of the Afrikaner Trekkers that I began to believe that their version of history entitled them to a privileged position in our country.

By early middle school, my aspirations began to be shaped by the crowned heads of European nobility who commissioned the Voyages of Discovery; the acrobatic skills of a Renaissance artist who whilst lying on his back had painted the magnificent fresco on the ceiling of the Sistine Chapel; and a small-town German monk who lit the flame of the Reformation by nailing his ninety-five theses onto the castle door in Wittenberg.

What would Herodotus, the father of history, make of this? Surely he never intended history to be solely the narrative of White men and the glorification of European exploits?

The history of people of color, their tragedies and triumphs, was distorted, erased, or hidden from our collective memory. We were deprived of the chance to see ourselves as pioneering explorers, imaginative innovators, or courageous leaders. Instead, we were taught that even a Black King needed to consume the gall of a White man so that he might gain courage.

I played on the revered grounds that had once belonged to Gandhi, plucked mangoes from the trees he planted, and attended the school he established, yet Gandhi was never the subject of my history lessons.

Finally, in sixth grade, the possibility of a hero that had been withheld came upon me unexpectedly.

A new boy arrived at school. At first I never saw him during breaks—neither on the playground, nor at the water tanks where a crowd always gathered, nor at any of the shady spots where lunch was eaten, scandals were stirred, and little gangs were formed to raid mango groves or sneak off to buy milk ice cubes from the houses outside the school boundary. I would learn soon enough that the new boy was Kidar, the great-grandson of Mahatma Gandhi.

When the Gandhi family returned to India, one of Gandhi's sons, Manilal Gandhi, who is Kidar's maternal grandfather, chose to stay in South Africa.

During the summer of 1974—at the height of the Cold War between the United States and the Soviet Union, and about a year after the famous chess championship between Boris Spassky and Bobby Fischer—Kidar and I finally got to know each other better.

It was a dark and gloomy day. Our school had no electricity, and on such days we were allowed to play board games. The captivating chess matches that had seized the world's attention had left a lasting impact on me. Now, even though I had not fully grasped the intricacies of chess, I too found myself fully immersed, strategizing opening moves and attempting tactical plays like castling and *en passant*.

Although Kidar claimed to have limited experience at chess, his remarkable knowledge suggested otherwise. I would soon discover that chess was a game of dualities, blending contradictory elements: black and white, art and science, a game played within the confines of a fixed geometric area yet offering an infinite number of possibilities. By midday, I found myself utterly perplexed, fixated on the white knight that Kidar skillfully maneuvered into position with its confounding

L-shaped jumps. So, imagine my relief and utter excitement when Kidar invited me to join him for lunch at his house.

I had long been curious about what lay beyond the permanently-locked wrought-iron gate, the brick retaining wall, and the mango groves that separated our classrooms from the sprawling property next door. Often I would sneak up to the gate and try to catch a glimpse of what was on the other side, but from my limited vantage point there wasn't much to see.

Kidar unlocked the neglected metal gate, and we strode past the printing press and 'Sarvodaya' (Gandhi's original home), and then along pathways bordered by manicured hedges, lemon trees, and recently-tilled rose gardens.

I had assumed that their home would be lavishly furnished, with all the trappings of wealth and status that came with being a descendant of the great Mahatma Gandhi. I pictured crystal chandeliers and teak tables with intricate ivory inlays of elephants in procession. But their home was nothing like what I had imagined. It was a modest farm-style dwelling that was spacious but simple.

We entered Kidar's home through the kitchen, and his dog Rajah was there to greet us. The aroma of dhal, bubbling on the kitchen stove, filled the air. I felt uneasy about arriving unannounced at lunchtime.

Kidar guided me to a low sofa positioned in the hallway, between the kitchen and the living-room. There were old portraits hanging on the wall. I was drawn towards one that depicted a distinguished gentleman, dressed formally in a suit and tie. His expression, though solemn, exuded charm and elegance. I assumed this was Gandhi, but I was not sure.

"Do you recognize this person?" Kidar asked.

"Is that your great-grandfather, Mahatma Gandhi?" I inquired.

"Yes, that's *Bapuji* (Great-Grandfather). It was taken when he qualified as a barrister in England."

As I examined the youthful portrait of Gandhi, it dawned upon me: If Helen of Troy is remembered as the face that launched a thousand ships, then Gandhi's charisma possessed the power to mobilize millions of people.

Kidar drew closer, raised his eyebrows twice, and whispered, "Can I share a little secret with you? While in England, *Bapuji* learned French, and even dabbled in ballroom dancing."

That's hilarious, I thought, my mind brimming with the image of an older Gandhi—clad in a loincloth, wire-rimmed glasses, sandals, and a walking stick—gracefully waltzing across the dance floor.

Another picture caught my attention—an image of Gandhi seated with an air of regal poise among a group of individuals, with a sign displaying "M. K. Gandhi, Attorney" in the background.

"Is this photograph taken in England?" I inquired.

"No, that one is from South Africa."

"But if he was a barrister in England, how did he end up in South Africa?"

"He came here to defend a client."

"Weren't there any lawyers here in South Africa?"

"He spoke Gujarati, the language of the merchant he was representing, and knew the intricacies of British law, under which the case was to be argued."

Kidar explained that after qualifying as a barrister in England, Gandhi returned to India. He was dissatisfied with the petty cases he handled there. Therefore he jumped at the opportunity to defend an Indian merchant who was involved in a civil lawsuit in South Africa.

"On the night before he was scheduled to leave South Africa, a farewell party was held to celebrate his winning the case," Kidar said.

During the event, someone presented him with a newspaper article detailing the British Government's intention to deprive Indians of their voting rights. The attendees pleaded that he stay for just one more month. That single month extended into twenty years, right here in the very spot where I now stood.

Though such a picture was not present on the wall, I had to ask about the famous train incident.

"My grandfather once told me that they threw your *Bapuji* off a train in Pietermaritzburg," I said.

"Ya, everyone knows that one. You know how stubborn *Bapuji* was," said Kidar. "Remember, *Bapuji* came from England, where professional Indian people didn't face as much discrimination as in South Africa."

Gandhi had purchased a first-class ticket and boarded a train bound for Pretoria. However, a White man objected to his presence in first class, and the ticket inspector reminded Gandhi that only White individuals were permitted in that section. He refused to leave and was forcibly thrown off the train at Pietermaritzburg station. That humiliation marked a turning point in his time in South Africa.

Gandhi witnessed the hardship faced by Indian people: their challenging living conditions, the unjust laws, and the imposition of the unethical three-pound poll tax. He was spat upon and called 'Coolie.' These experiences led him to acknowledge the profound inequality between White and Indian people in South Africa. A fresh approach was required to confront the might of colonial power. It was this realization that gave birth to *Satyagraha*: a philosophy that was centered around nonviolence but that encouraged deliberate acts of civil disobedience.

The skills and strategies honed during his experiences in South Africa proved to be crucial when Gandhi returned to India. His remarkable ability to rally people round a shared cause played a pivotal role in ultimately securing India's liberation from British rule.

That day I received far more than I had expected. Not only was I granted a meaningful history lesson, but it would also mark my initiation into the realm of political activism in South Africa.

Kidar's parents had come home, and Rajah was barking and spinning around in joyous circles at the front door.

"My parents are still banned, you know. They're back from reporting at the police station, something that they must do every day," said Kidar.

Mr. Ramgobind, Kidar's father, presented the outward appearance of a stern and austere man, the result of many years of hostile confrontation with the authorities. He had close-cropped black hair, wore dark glasses, and sported a well-cut suit that was tailored from the kind of fabric that made you want to reach out and touch it.

Aunty Ela, Kidar's mother, was a social worker. From her fluting voice, and a personality that was filled with humility, one might not have guessed that Aunty Ela had a rebellious streak. Behind her sweet, dark eyes and winsome smile lay a gleam of mischief, and the tenacity of a tiger.

Aunty Ela observed me carefully. "You look just like your mother," she said. Her eyes sparkled with recognition, and a girlish, giggly smile crossed her face as she recalled the memory of being in primary school with my mom.

"I'm sorry for bothering you during lunch, Aunty Ela."

"Don't apologize, dear. I'm happy you came," she replied warmly.

Kidar's parents' movements were severely restricted: they were under perpetual house arrest, and were not allowed to attend any gathering where there were more than two people. Kidar told me later about the many times they heard alarming noises in the dead of night. In one such incident, at 3 a.m., the police smashed their way through the front door, toppled the furniture, emptied drawers, and even tore apart the sofas in the living-room. I wondered how they managed to live under such constant fear.

After lunch, Kidar and I accompanied his dad into the sitting-room, which led out into a sprawling garden.

"It's truly remarkable," exclaimed Mr. Ramgobind, his voice brimming with excitement. A minute of silence ensued, and I waited to hear what was so remarkable.

"Do you know the origin of chess?" he asked.

"No, Uncle Mewa," I said.

"Chess is an Indian game. Let me show you how to play the Maharajah and the Sepoys."

Kidar brought out a much larger board, and Mr. Ramgobind arranged all the black pieces in the usual way and then placed the white king alone, in its normal position, on the opposite side.

My hopes were high, now that I was to be presented with something out of the ordinary. Though I dared not speak up, I was inwardly convinced that there was an errant spark of mischief in this setup.

With absolute assurance shining in his face, Mr. Ramgobind said, "Yes, I know just what you're thinking. Chess is a game with clearly defined rules. There's no rolling of dice or drawing of cards. What you see is fair, because the white king has the privilege of moving as any of the black pieces: as queen, rook, bishop, or even the knight."

That was a peculiar and intriguing perspective on a game that I was just beginning to comprehend. At that time, I did not understand the symbolic element that he presented that day. I grasped the concept that *Maharajah* referred to an Indian King, but to unravel the meaning of *sepoy*, I had to turn to the pages of the *Oxford English Dictionary*. There I discovered that a *sepoy* denoted an Indian soldier who served under the command of a British or European officer.

The history lesson that Mr. Ramgobind alluded to in the Maharajah and the Sepoys was perhaps a lesson that held relevance for a future time, and emphasized a reversal of fortunes, rather than servitude. I was fixated in the history of the present, trapped in the knowledge that my position in our society was in the middle, caught between White people at the top and Black people below. After learning the meaning of *sepoy*, I applied it in a literal sense: Indian and African people serving White people, and African people serving Indian people.

CHAPTER 7

1949

More than a hundred years after their arrival in South Africa, not a single Indian person worked in the sugarcane fields. After all that time, and true to the label of *sepoys*, Indians were viewed as people who were serving the interest of their White masters, and were accused of colluding with them to undermine African aspirations.

Indian people played the role of the middleman. They were the clerks and the managers who ran the operations of White businesses, the foremen who shouted orders to the African laborers, and the chargehands who pushed them to work faster and longer. Moreover, many Indian people employed African people to do the menial tasks that they were not prepared to do—as house servants, laborers in construction sites, and garden 'boys'.

We could not afford a maid, but we often employed African men to help with the gardening.

One spring morning, in September of 1974, I watched the garden boy through the open sitting-room window. He had finished slashing down the grass, which had grown tall following a season of rainstorms, and was hunched over on his knees, turning the soil and removing weeds from the flower bed. The air was filled with the loamy scent of freshly-tilled earth that teemed with wriggly worms.

Thatha towered over the man's arched body. "Only the weeds, *mfana* (young man), not the flower plants," he said.

"*Ai, suka*," said the garden boy, gesturing that Thatha should go away.

A bumblebee buzzed about the garden boy's head, but he kept his gaze rooted in the dirt, his arms moving with mechanical monotony. I'm sure he understood Thatha's instructions, but the words seemed to whizz right past his consciousness, his face showing nothing other than a mask of defiance.

Thatha kept a close eye on the garden boy. It was more than just observing. Thatha was watching him like a hawk hovering overhead, his eyes darting swiftly, scanning, tracking the garden boy's every move. He constantly shifted positions, getting closer, then quickly sidestepping or backing away as though he needed to make a hasty retreat. I was unable to discern the nature of Thatha's agitation, but all that vigilance suggested that what he saw in the garden boy's hands was not a trowel, but a *panga* (machete), and that at any moment he expected this warrior to rise and attack him.

I yearned to know what was going on inside their heads, to understand this mysterious tension between Thatha and the garden boy.

Meanwhile, Ama busied herself with her customary Friday chores: washing the prayer lamps, polishing the brass ornaments, and adorning the front doorway with a fresh garland of marigolds. Just as I made a move to sneak out into the garden, she reminded me that the polish on the verandah floor had dried.

I skidded and slid along the red cement floor, sliding and swaying as I shone it smooth with a foot brush.

The garden boy spotted me and burst into hysterical laughter, convinced that I was possessed by an evil spirit. "*Uyasangana*! (You're crazy!)," he said.

I retreated behind the front door, closing it just enough so that he would not be able to mistake the value of our modest belongings: cheap lace curtains that came by the bale, papier-mâché Indian dolls with bobbing heads and wobbly waists, dusty bouquets of colorful plastic flowers, and a sideboard adorned with a parade of glittering brass elephants, rabbits, and ducks.

He appeared more at ease now that he had settled down on the cool verandah floor. Perhaps it was a reprieve from the scorching midday sun, or the anticipation of lunch, but more likely it was I who experienced a sense of relief, knowing that the garden boy posed less of a threat now that he was seated.

Ama asked me to fetch the enamel plate and plastic tumbler from under the kitchen sink. She served the leftover mutton curry with a thick slice of buttered bread. I stood behind the safety of the part of Ama's sari that draped loosely over her shoulder, and observed the glee with which the garden boy awaited his meal.

"*Nyama* (meat)," Ama said, her tone coaxing gratitude.

"*Ngiyabonga* (thank you)," he said. He nodded in appreciation, turning his eyes downwards and away from Ama. In his culture it was disrespectful to look the speaker in the eye.

The riots of 1949 were a secret, '1949' used only as an allusion. When I was a child, I often wondered why we regarded African men with such suspicion. I had a strong feeling it was somehow connected to 1949. There were several times that I had overheard adults in my family speak about '1949', in hushed tones and after we had gone to bed. It sounded as though what they were discussing was too terrible, even within their restricted circle. Whenever I approached, they would stop talking, or switch the conversation to something else.

Once, I had asked Ama about 1949, and a bolt of panic rushed across her face. She was cooking that afternoon, and I was doing my homework at the kitchen table. Ama was typically forthright, even with the most uncomfortable questions. Yet, on this occasion, while she did not evade my enquiry, she appeared hesitant and unable to paint a cohesive picture of her experience.

"It happened a long time ago," she said. Her tone was steady and neutral. "I was only nine then, and all I can remember was more a feeling of fear than any of the actual details."

"What were you afraid of, Ma?" I asked.

"I don't know," she said. "Just fear."

Then, sometime in the autumn of 1975, the facts about 1949 were inadvertently revealed to me. I should not have eavesdropped, but that was the only way to discover the truth. The things I heard were not simply a reimagining of an event in the distant past. I was struck by the immediacy of it all, as though it were happening at that very moment, told by people who were bearing witness to the situation in real time.

On a Sunday afternoon, after church was done, Thatha's cousin Joseph Mama and his wife arrived in their green Morris Minor. Joseph Mama was a precise little man, short in stature, with white hair that was swept gently back, and as a person in his late sixties, his face was just beginning to show signs of aging. He spoke fluently, with gravity, and once he got into his oratorical stride, he enunciated with preacher-like authority. His wife, Aunty Daphne, was a 'Coloured' lady, an earthy woman with an uncensored flair for speaking her mind. She wore flat shoes and simple dresses with drab floral patterns. In the strict sense of apartheid laws, their marriage was illegal, but the authorities sometimes overlooked mixed marriages between people of color.

Thatha took his cousin on a tour of the garden, taking pride in showcasing our chili-pepper bushes, the double beans on vines that grew in uniform rows, calabashes, and watercress herbs. It satisfied him that Joseph Mama inspected each plant with the same care and detail as an art lover would appraise the *Mona Lisa*. They plucked carrots and radishes, and pinched off a few green chilies. These fresh ingredients would later be grated, chopped, diced, and drizzled with vinegar, providing a zesty accompaniment to the ill-fated, red-crested rooster which Poobal and I had chased down in the chicken coop.

After lunch, the men retired to the sitting-room and settled down on the old-fashioned mahogany sofa.

Joseph Mama massaged his tummy. "Ah, that was one helluva chicken curry," he said.

"Nothing beats 'running fowl' for a good chicken curry," Thatha said.

"*Maam* (*Maama*), our old ways are dying. Everyone wants the easy life now. It's just so convenient to buy these pigeon-sized Rainbow chickens from the store."

"Yes, Joseph, time is flying by, and we must make the best of what's left."

Thatha walked over to the dresser. "What'll you have, Joseph?"

"Oh, the usual, Maam."

Thatha poured a shot of Joseph Mama's preferred spirit, the sugarcane-based Mainstay.

"You know, Maam, this week, the United Nations called apartheid a crime against humanity," Joseph Mama said.

"Really? I hadn't heard that," Thatha said.

"We're living in a new world now. African people don't listen to us the way they used to," Joseph Mama said.

Thatha turned, half facing Joseph Mama, a frown coming over his face. "Just the other day, I asked the garden boy to avoid pulling out the young marigolds. You know what he said? '*Ai, suka.*' The damn cheek to ask me to go away!"

"Do you think we'll see the day when they will come to power?"

"I don't know, Joseph. This country belongs to them."

"But we were born here. This is our country too," Joseph Mama said. He shifted uncomfortably, unsettled by the absurdity, the sheer foolishness of the idea.

Thatha took a sip of his brandy and sighed. "We're stuck in the middle. White people use us as shields, while African people see us as wheelers and dealers. At the first hint of trouble, African people will turn against us."

"Jesus Christ, that would be like 1949 happening all over again." Joseph Mama almost jumped out of his seat, the pitch in his voice rising in disbelief.

Aunty Daphne's cheeks flushed with anger. She had been listening carefully, and like a pressure-cooker that had reached the point of explosion, she could stay silent no more. "Why do you have to talk about bloody politics, Joe! What good will come of this? All you do is scare the children."

Joseph Mama looked downwards, crippled by doubt, and, like a child who had been admonished, he regretted having spoken at all. For a few moments, both men sat in quiet contemplation.

The siege of silence continued. A lizard peeked out from the air vent, enticed by a fly that was struggling on the glue-ribbon trap that hung from the ceiling board. Joseph Mama looked weary, as though the privacy of his soul was invaded, like he possessed some terrible secret but was unsure whether he should divulge it.

Joseph Mama sighed, his voice radiating a solemn sincerity. "You know, my sister's husband died in the Cato Manor riots of 1949."

Thatha put his hands on his cousin's shoulder. "This must be painful for you, Joseph. We don't have to talk about it," he said.

There was more silence, time enough for me to absorb the gravity of what was unfolding before me. Hearing words like "this country belongs to them," "riots," some relative dead, and just the date, 1949, made my skin crawl and sent a shiver up my spine. It was in these private moments that Thatha's voice held just a hint of fear, a foreboding, that someday African people would reclaim what was rightfully theirs. At a time when I was still struggling to come to terms with my own apprehension towards African people, hearing Thatha speak that way rekindled the fear of *bululu bambas* carrying me off in a sack.

Joseph Mama was undaunted, and, as painful as it appeared, he wanted to speak, to unburden himself of the trauma that was concealed within. Slowly, he began to unwrap the layers of the emotional shroud that bound his fears.

"Booth Road was such a vibrant place in those days. Indian and African people lived side by side. On some Sundays when I visited my sister, I would see African men stumbling back from the beerhalls in Cato Manor. You know, Maam, our Indian bus drivers and conductors were nasty to them."

"Yes, the buses did not even wait for the men, they rolled by and left many African men stranded in the exhaust fumes," Thatha said.

"You know, some of our chaps did not even give a ticket to those who entered through the door at the back," Joseph Mama said.

"And to top it all, the conductors in front would accuse the blokes of not paying, and whip them," Thatha said.

Booth Road, in Cato Manor, lay on the outskirts of Durban. The community had a unique mix of residents. Indian landlords rented out parts of their farms to African women and children. Under apartheid laws, only African men were given *dompasses* to live in urban areas. But their families wanted to get away from the hardships of rural life and be closer to their menfolk, so they settled on the fringes of the city. It was a kind of secret deal, because these sub-letting arrangements were also against the law.

On weekends, the African men abandoned the confined spaces of their urban hostels and escaped to the vibrant beerhalls of Cato Manor, where music, food, and women abounded. After a few days of revelry, the men would stagger towards the bus stop.

There was more silence, more contemplation. Then the gory details emerged, little by little, like priceless ancient artifacts, delicately uncovered by an archaeologist.

"Poor man, my brother-in-law, he was in town when the trouble started," said Joseph Mama.

"To think that an argument over one cigarette could cause such tragedy," Thatha added.

The *Indian Opinion* reported the incident on its front page: "The riots were sparked by an argument that arose between fourteen-year-old George Madondo and a shop assistant, Dhanraj, over a cigarette. Madondo slapped Dhanraj, causing the owner of the shop to push Madondo through a glass window."

"I remember, it was a Thursday afternoon in January of 1949. My brother-in-law was waiting for his bus in Victoria Street. You know how busy the Indian area is at five o'clock: the dock workers rushing back to their hostels, shopkeepers closing up, and the traffic is just crazy at that time," Joseph Mama said.

"I misunderstood you, Joseph. I didn't realize that your brother-in-law actually saw the trouble?"

"Yes, Maam, he was in the middle of it. The African ladies across the street began ululating. You know how that gets their men all worked up and ready for action? Anyhow, before he knew it, stones and bottles came raining down on them and he had to run for his life."

"That sounds horrible. I also remember reading about that in the *Indian Opinion*," Thatha said.

The newspaper characterized the shopkeeper's actions as "a few insignificant slaps," and portrayed photographs of African youths whom the paper described as "violent young African men hurling missiles with grins on their faces and a strange, possessed light in their eye." It went on to report that all along the Indian area in Grey Street, the shoe stores and sari shops, the spice houses and restaurants were smashed open and ransacked. An African rickshaw puller even loaded his vehicle with armloads of shoes. There were sheets, blankets, and clothing of every sort strewn about the street.

"It is strange, Joseph, how one man's actions caused so many Africans to declare war on Indians."

Whether it was a push, a shove, a jostle, or a forceful thrust, the magnitude of the assault seemed insufficient to ignite a riot, especially in a time when African people exhibited a sense of 'obedience' that rarely questioned the actions of Indian individuals. Perhaps it was the shocking sight of an adult assaulting a fourteen-year-old boy, the shattering sound of breaking glass, or the haunting image of blood staining the pavement that triggered such a unified and resolute reaction.

What Thatha and Joseph Mama failed to grasp was the decades of pent-up resentment against a community of immigrants who were regarded as snobbish and exploitative. While all non-White individuals were subordinate to their White masters, African people found it particularly offensive to witness Indian people assuming the role of non-White masters.

Joseph Mama continued, and each unwinding of that story, every strip that was ripped off, served only to resurrect the skeletons of the past. I was awestruck, shocked by the uncomfortable knowledge that pulsed beneath his words. They still had no idea that I was listening. As afraid as I was, I needed to hear it all.

"You know how these guys like to blow things out of proportion? Each time, they made the story look much worse. First they accused the shopkeeper of *smashing* the boy's head against the window. They even claimed that the liquor sold by Indians caused TB, and that VD amongst Africans was the result of Indian men going after African women," Joseph Mama said.

"That's ridiculous," Thatha said.

"That's not the worst of it. By Friday afternoon, when the young African boy was doing well in hospital, rumors spread through the hostels. Now, they claimed that his head was cut off and put on display in the Indian mosque on Grey Street."

"Oh God! There's nothing that can rile African people more than the power of *muti* or black magic," Thatha said.

"They man-handled our people in the streets, Maam, robbed them of their wages, and hit them with *knobkerries*. At the Top Market Rank, bus conductors were whipped and hacked with *pangas* (machetes), and their buses were set alight," Joseph Mama said.

Joseph Mama's voice trembled, and every now and then a twitch came over his chin. His hands seemed unable to rest quietly, and he cleared his throat more frequently. Clearly, he had never been able to overcome the trauma of 1949. The fear that rippled through his words sent tremors vibrating through my bones.

"That evening, the armed hostel dwellers made their way out of the city center and towards Cato Manor," Joseph Mama said. "The Indian people in Cato Manor had no chance, Maam. There were no police to protect them. They looted and burnt, looted and burnt—everything around my sister's home was scorched."

"And what about your sister's family, Joseph?"

"My brother-in-law stayed behind to protect the house. My sister and the children ran through the banana groves and climbed up into the mango trees. You know, my sister was so afraid that her shrieks would give up their position that she actually stuffed the end of her sari into her mouth. From up in the trees they watched flames leaping out of their home and heard terrifying screams coming from inside."

Joseph Mama's words came out in fits and starts now, and it cost him a terrible effort to reach past the relentless pain that was trapped in his soul.

"At sunrise…when things became silent…they came down from the trees. They found my brother-in-law…He was dead…lying like a dog on the street outside. Their home was burnt. My poor sister, what could she do?"

In the days that followed, before I went to bed, I checked that the front and back doors were properly locked, and even pulled on the burglar guards to make sure they were secure. I got up in the middle of the night, listening for sounds that were unusual, checking the windows to make sure that no intruder was standing outside. There were times when Thatha had to nudge me awake so that I would stop grinding my teeth. My dreams—no, they were not dreams, my nightmares—were filled with horrific scenes of houses engulfed in flames, the screams of desperate people trapped inside, of men lying in the street with their skulls splayed open, dying like convulsing rabid dogs.

CHAPTER 8

The Risk of Ruin

The Michaelmas holidays had ended, and we were in the first few days of the last school term in October of 1974. I was doing my homework at the kitchen table when a frightening cry broke the silence. I dropped my pen and rushed over to the prayer room, from where I suspected the sound had come.

My entire family was gathered there, standing to attention as if they were in a police identity lineup. Thatha stood before the queue. He had the face of one who could walk through fire: his mouth contorted into a fierce grimace, his eyes wide and bloodshot, and his tongue protruding through teeth that were tightly clenched. In his right hand, he held a long-bladed knife.

For a wild moment—with my recently acquired knowledge of 1949, the screams, the fires, the *panga*s, and seeing Thatha in this terrifying state—the idea came to me that we were under attack by African tribesmen who were plundering through Duffs Road. Was Thatha responding to their ancestral spirits by drumming up some kind of black magic of our own?

"It's only a trance," Ama said. "Sometimes Thatha turns into the fierce image of Madurai Veeran." (Madurai Veeran is a guardian god of Tamil Nadu state in India.)

If it was only a trance, as Ama claimed, then why were those in the queue trembling so much, I thought.

The trance stood before Dad. It appeared more menacing, its fury heightened as the supernatural attempted to bend the future. Dad quivered, his jaw dropped, the perspiration that had gathered along his hairline was now streaming down his temples. He gave a solemn assurance, "I won't go to the races anymore, Naina. I promise. I promise, Naina."

My father was a gambling man. He was tethered to the sport of kings, and how thrilled he was to be in the glamorous company of royalty.

"Just you wait and see," he would say, "one day my luck will change, and I will hit the jackpot." He was blinkered by an unwavering belief that in a single sweep, his windfall would compensate for all the financial hardship of his difficult life.

On Friday nights Dad brought home the weekend race card. He called it 'the Bible.' With the help of the form guide in the *Daily News,* and the Bible, we had everything that was required for Saturday's horse racing. Dad took great pride in teaching my brother Poobal and me how to analyze the odds by paying careful attention to the fine details. We knew that *Gatecrasher* came from the stables of Herman Brown, that *Sentinel* was unbeatable in a sprint of 1,000 meters, and that the track conditions would be yielding after heavy rains. We never gambled, but on special days like the Durban July Handicap, Dad would place a bet in our name.

Sometimes Dad took the whole family to the racecourse. While he spent the day punting, Ama sat with us in the car outside the track at Greyville. We munched on peanuts that were freshly roasted in their shells as we watched the horses trot up to the start. There was a wild energy as the hooves of reluctant horses kicked up dust while jockeys tried to coax the horses into the stalls. I felt a pure adrenaline rush when the gates sprang open. The finish line was a thousand meters down, too far to see who had won, but we cheered them all, hoping that Dad had backed the winner.

As the hours passed, I would feed another five-cent coin into the parking meter, and when there were no more coins to find in the cubby (glove compartment), or under the mats, I would step out and try to exchange a one-rand note (about US $1 at the time) for more coins. The African lady who sold steamed bread called *dombolos* was hesitant to give me change. Although Ama disapproved of buying food from street vendors, I sometimes had no choice but to purchase a *dombolo*. On one of those days, I held up a five-cent coin and marveled at it as though it held some strange power. I vowed to save up those coins until they amounted to a rand, and then I would continue to save those rands. That day, I promised myself that I would never gamble, and that I would hold on to every bit of small change.

In late October or November of 1974, luck smiled upon my father, and he won some money at the races. He always dreamt of visiting the revered mountaintop temple in Tamil Nadu state in India, after which he was named 'Palani'. Like the spiritual appeal of the Holy Land for Christians, or Mecca for Muslims, Palani Malai held a special place in the hearts of Tamils. He decided to take us all along—Thatha and Ama; me (thirteen); Poobal (eleven); my two younger sisters, Devi (eight) and Thiliga (six); and our youngest sibling, Ron, who was only six months old.

Dad wasted no time in planning the trip. Tickets were purchased, passports applied for, and before we knew it we were all receiving our yellow-fever shots at the Department of Indian Affairs. A week later we were on the tarmac at Louis Botha Airport in Durban, waiting to board our propeller jet plane BOAC (British Overseas Airways Corporation) flight to India.

Poobal and I could not contain our excitement. It was our first time on an airplane, and in an era when air travel was uncommon we felt like celebrities. Thatha even had suits specially tailored for us. On December 2, 1974, we bid farewell to over fifty friends and relatives who had gathered to see us off.

In India we visited the Taj Mahal, the Gateway to India, and the palaces and forts of Rajasthan. But there was no place that moved Dad as much as Palani Malai. An elderly devotee sang hymns in praise of the deity, drums beat, bells clanged, incense rose in clouds, and there was a collective chant of '*Muruga, Muruga, Muruga*' (Tamil god). My father was transported into an ethereal state, convinced that he must endure the penance of carrying *kavady* (a weight carried on the shoulder).

Poobal and Dad shaved the hair off their scalps, smeared sacred sandalwood paste on their heads, and wrapped loincloths around their waists. Then they hoisted the twenty-kilogram semicircular *kavady*—decorated with flowers and peacock feathers—and carried it up the 670 stone steps to the temple at the top. I was too proud, too self-conscious, to shave off my hair and be part of the ritual. I joined the rest of the family and took the winch train up to the temple.

As we waited for Poobal and Dad, I gulped down milk that was offered in prayer; cardamon-flavored, with chopped pieces of banana. I secretly hoped that Dad's penance and this ambrosia of the gods would help him to stop gambling.

While we were away in India, some of the elders in our family held a meeting. For a long time they'd had it in their minds that all our troubles were owing to my father's gambling. They argued that he would be more responsible if he were to manage his affairs outside our communal home in Duffs Road.

Thatha was not happy, especially given that a decision was taken in his absence. In the months following our return from India, a feeling of oppression settled over our household in Duffs Road. Food was cooked separately, and supper was eaten in silence. People passed each other without saying "good morning." It was an awkward time for a child to be stuck in the middle. I could feel the hurt that was consuming Thatha, but what could he do?

Ama was pregnant again, with my sister Judy, who was due five months later, in February of 1976. With a tender tone, and in the privacy of their bedroom, Dad promised Ama that he would abandon his gambling, that life would be better in the future. He suggested the many benefits of moving to Verulam, a town about thirty kilometers up the North Coast from Duffs Road.

"Verulam has a great high school. Think about how much that would improve Krish's chance of getting into medical school," Dad said.

In March of 1976, soon after Judy was born, Ama, Dad, and the six of us kids left behind the house of my childhood. I was heartbroken, for there are no memories more precious than those from early childhood in one's first home. Being torn away from Thatha under such cruel circumstances cast a shadow over my days. Helpless and lonely, I felt a profound sense of loss, cut off from the security of the world as I knew it. I yearned for the comfort and wisdom that Thatha had always given me.

Verulam was a town of twenty thousand people, situated among rolling hills of sugarcane. During apartheid it was zoned as an Indian area.

If you strolled through Verulam on a Saturday morning you would most likely encounter the huge crowds that are drawn to the outdoor farmer's market. The air would be filled with the chatter of people haggling with gardeners, interrupted only by the siren of the noon-train as it crossed the iron bridge over the Umdloti River before passing alongside the market. If you walked a little further, up towards the center of town and the intersection of Wick and Moss streets, you would notice Asmal's and Bomvane's, clothing stores where we went for back-to-school shopping, and Razak's Butchery, from where we got our spicy mutton sausages. From the corner of your eye you would have espied the Luxmi Theatre, that on weekends showed double-feature Indian movies. As your gaze rose and fell, you would see the minarets and domes of the Verulam Mosque on Wick Street, and recognize the Moulana's call to midday prayer. Further up Wick Street you would come upon the Green Cat Complex, where Bruce Lee's *Enter the Dragon* dominated the box office that year. Next door you would have heard the incoherent murmur of drunks stumbling out of the Starlite Bar, and horse racing commentary blaring from loudspeakers at Tattersall's.

The house we rented, at the gravel-patch end of Garden Street, was on a property that was shared by a rotating cast of families. The space we sought came in an abundance of rooms with cheerfully creaky wooden floors, and warped windows that favored the draught that often fluttered through. The lightbulbs hung naked from cords that sagged off stained ceiling-boards. Whenever it rained, old buckled pots, used Rama margarine containers, and plastic buckets were strategically positioned to collect the water that dripped in through the leaky roof. We lined up each morning, towel in hand, to share the single outdoor toilet and bathroom.

Three months after we moved to Verulam, on June 16, 1976, to be precise, several groups of African students from high schools in Soweto (the SOuth WEstern TOwnships) began to march to protest a new law that mandated Afrikaans as the language of instruction in all African schools. The day would turn out to be a 'where were you' moment, similar to the assassination of JFK or the collapse of the Twin Towers in New York.

I cannot recall with any degree of certainty what I was doing on that Wednesday, six hundred kilometers away from the action. It was most likely an ordinary school day. While the students were marching and singing freedom songs, carrying crudely scrawled placards that read *Away with Afrikaans*, I was probably walking up Garden Street towards my new school in Everest Heights. When the police suddenly opened fire on the students in Soweto, leaving bodies scattered in the dusty streets, I would have been sitting through my Afrikaans lesson. And when photographer Sam Nzima hid the unfinished spool that held the iconic image of a lifeless thirteen-year-old being carried along, the focus of my lunchtime was adjusting to a newfound fascination with breasts and bras.

As the country plunged into chaos, unbeknownst to me, my life was also careening down a tumultuous path. Dad's gambling got worse, and now that he was free from Thatha's watchful eye, his license knew no bounds. Even in his sleep he would mumble numbers, call out the names of horses, and sometimes mimic tearing up losing betting stubs and flinging them into the air.

Dad's addiction to gambling was too strong for him to overcome. He was driven by the thrill of winning, the sense of control and power it provided, and the rush of adrenaline that came with each successful bet. Each time he struggled to claw his way out of the spiraling vortex of addiction, he found himself drawn deeper and deeper into its grip, until finally, he succeeded only in falling back into its depths and being devoured by it.

Month after month Dad's paycheck seemed to vanish. Even during the festive season, when we anticipated a little extra, we were left disappointed and empty-handed. One Christmas, instead of bearing gifts, Dad came home with a nasty scalp wound. He claimed to have been robbed. As I watched the doctor stitch up his gash, I wondered if there was more to the story than he was letting on. These were questions that no child should ever grapple with, and it was heartbreaking to see his suffering.

He was helpless. I was helpless. We were all helpless.

Ama became more withdrawn. I could see it in her constant brooding, her vacant gaze, and her repetitive rocking motion. She argued their marriage to near extinction, for lengthy periods and late into the night. Perhaps they felt like hermits in a sealed echo-chamber: but we could hear it all. Although I never saw her tears, the morning would present evidence that left little doubt: darkly circled eyes, a disconsolately drawn face, and the exhausted frown of one defeated. Then there were those weeks when Ama assumed a pledge of silence. I was not sure which was worse.

I am not entirely certain, but at times I wonder if Ama used food as a deliberate tactic to garner our sympathy. For days we would have to endure the same mixed-vegetable curry, a thin and tasteless gravy filled with string beans, diced carrots, peas, and chopped potatoes. Chunks of cheap, pink-dyed mutton polony, packed in between thickly-sliced buttered bread, became my comfort food.

Sometime later, on a Saturday usually, I would watch Ama gather spices, toast them in the oven, and grind them all with mortar and pestle. The fragrant oils filled the kitchen with a soothing scent. That evening, the return of steaming-hot chicken biryani—made with layers of black lentils, rice infused with saffron, Cornish hen cooked in the fragrant spices and garnished with butter-sautéed onions—signaled to all that peace had finally been restored.

Dad was charming, because that's how addicts are. When he was around people, he was always smiling and could talk his way out of any situation. One July Handicap Day, I remember Dad's friends arriving to escort him to the premiere event in the racing calendar. The Durban July was a gala event, an occasion for fancy clothes, where the ladies donned hats adorned with feathers and blooms. Dad wore a stylish suit and tie that day, but inadvertently put on a pair of mismatched, brightly-colored socks. His friends broke into laughter. Instead of being embarrassed, Dad turned on the charisma and said, "It's my secret lucky charm."

Then, on a quiet Sunday morning, I would find my father seated alone on the front verandah, the morning breeze carrying whispers of regret and missed opportunities. A tattered racing program would be spread open on his lap, his infectious laugh replaced by sighs, his eyes wandering into the distance and lost in a sea of what-ifs. I could see the pain in his naturally kind face, the expression of suffering and solemn resignation that was eroding his being. Such moments brought me to the realization that no matter what, I could never be angry with Dad.

Dad built defenses like the Romans built forts: not as convincingly solid structures, but more as wispy pillars of fantasy. He lived in a world that was of his own making and accessible only to him. And in his world, if ever there was a three-legged horse in a race, Dad would not hesitate to put money on it, and not because he thought it would win. He would have said, "Imagine how glorious it would be if it did win!" All reason was sacrificed on the altar of his delusional thinking.

Dad knew how to bargain, because addicts are experts at bargaining. Sometimes he retreated into almost total silence; and then there were other times when he would slide out from under his shell, ready to crucify himself for his ingratitude. He would snuggle up on the sofa beside Ama, put his arm around her shoulder, give a gentle squeeze, and say, "*Cattiyama* (power to truth)," and pledge to stay away from the horses. While Dad had the habit of forgetting too quickly, Ama never forgot anything. There were times when she might have given in to his cajoling, but I wonder how deeply hurt she must have been, and how harshly she must have looked upon him during those moments.

The playground of the children who lived in our shared yard, where Garden Street ended at Booth Road, was an area that was adjacent to a dimly lit 'shebeen,' an illegal drinking establishment. It was a place where hooded young men took long drags of marijuana through makeshift pipes that were fashioned by breaking a glass beer-bottle at its neck. It would have been so easy to become bitter about the cards that life had dealt me, mired in self-indulgent pity, and resentful as to the unfairness of my father's misdeeds that were so cruelly visited upon me. I, too, could have descended into that Booth Road kind of life.

I carried my emotions like a private ache. These were issues that were part of my life, that required resolution on my terms, and without blaming others. On weekends, I spent hours wandering along the serene country path that led away from our home and into the grassy valley that ends at the Umdloti River. All the while I pretended that I was meandering through the English countryside, imagining the dandelions as daffodils, listening to the rustle of leaves in the trees, and feeling the gentle caress of a breeze on my face. It was in these moments that I discovered a sense of calm, a private space where I could process my emotions without burdening others.

Just when I believed that I was handling my feelings quite well, the weight of that psychological strife broke me, slowly at first, then steadily. The world around me turned dull and grey. Each day felt like an insurmountable battle. Sleep eluded me, and my nights were plagued with restless tossing and turning. I struggled to find purpose and meaning, and the path to becoming a doctor, once filled with promise, was overtaken by anxiety and insecurity.

There was just no money for new clothes, or even a haircut. Ama did her best to cut my hair, but she often cropped off too much, and cut my bangs in an uneven wisp that curled irritatingly up my forehead. My single pair of school pants, though worn and in parts threadbare, had to last the entire year. It did not matter that my thighs, fattened by too much mutton polony, had fashioned a hole on the inner side of the trousers. I had the constant fear that the defect in my pants would deprive me of my dignity, and I took every measure to conceal it. People notice things like unevenly-cut hair, a bulge in a seam, and the pucker of a pleat. I was forever conscious that they were aware, and that made me feel shabby. Feeling shabby stifled me, forced me to become preoccupied with anticipating every potential humiliation, and slashed my confidence.

Like any teenager, I wanted to be loved for being perfect. My desire for affection and inclusiveness was no less than anyone else's. I dreamt that I would meet someone, someone who would be in awe of me, and that I would present myself at her door someday and claim her adoration. But I was not blessed with good looks or charisma, had neither money nor fancy clothes, and lived in a house that ought to have been condemned. I swooned with shame, and suffered the painful paralysis that accompanies the fear of being mocked or rejected. What chance did I have of making the acquaintance of any girl? Who would even consider going out with me? On the last day of school, while many of my classmates planned to boogie under the glitterball at the Starlight nightclub, I slouched homewards and resigned myself to an unmarketable fate.

In high school, we studied Shakespeare's *Hamlet*. It was perhaps inevitable that I came to see myself in the tragic hero archetype of the protagonist. Like Hamlet, I deceived myself by putting on an antic disposition of sorts. I assumed an outward mantle of bravado and tried to wall off a protected space, fortifying myself against the ridicule of other people's judgements. I resolved that I was not worthy of any girl's affection, that such feelings were not intended for me. By keeping rejection at arm's length, I believed that I could avoid it altogether. Yet my inner self both yearned for and mistrusted closeness. The detachment for which I strove made me suffer from too much of it.

I became lost in the all-consuming project of shaping a version of myself that people might see from the outside and admire, and through admiring, come to love me. All my energy was committed to being the best at everything that I undertook. I hoped that someone—no, not just someone, but everyone—would see what I had achieved, and see me in the way I wanted to be seen, and love me for it. Who would not want that? That is the kind of yearning that we are born with, and that is the kind of yearning that many will die without fulfilling.

Money—getting it, losing it, never having enough of it—ran through our lives like a watermark through a ten-rand note. During the summer of my grade eleven year, I felt compelled to go out in search of work. I went to Repsta, a business that made school stationery—part-owned by a classmate's father. They offered me a packing job. I felt embarrassed, but was willing to take it.

Ama was furious and would have none of it.

"I'll work harder if I must, but I will not have you work," she said. She believed that the short-term lure of easy money would distract me from the path of becoming a doctor.

By the end of that week, Ama had purchased an Elna flatbed knitting machine. It was bought on credit that was to be paid off with money from the sari blouses that she would sell. On Saturdays, as she haggled with sellers and filled her basket with vegetables from the Verulam Farmer's Market, she showed samples and took orders for knitted blouses. She marked the orders in a little black book, using uncanny descriptive names to identify her clients.

"Why do you write such funny names in the order book?" I once asked her.

"How else will I remember who the order belongs to," she said.

"I understand Lady under the Tree and Beetle Nut Aunty, but who is Gravy Soaker Amoi?"

"Don't you know? She's the aunty who sells those soft cooking potatoes."

As the number of orders increased, our list of chores grew. As the mechanical carriage screeched through rows of needles, my sisters, Thiliga and Devi, assisted with the dishes, while Poobal and I hung the washed clothes on the lines outside. On Friday nights, now that we were freed from Dad's 'Bible studies,' my sister Devi and I stitched the sleeves onto the blouses so that the orders would make it out on time for the Saturday morning market.

It was difficult to imagine how my situation could get any worse, but it did. My illness started gradually, with a vague feeling of malaise. Then came the burning fever and diarrhea, and soon my eyes turned yellow, my head ached, and I faltered like a newborn giraffe. I put it down to eating too many loquats. The doctor said it was yellow jaundice. It did not carry the same metaphorical weight as double pneumonia, but it sounded important enough to justify the few weeks that I would miss school. There was no special treatment. I needed time to rest, lots of it.

Ama could not wait. She pinned her hopes on the doubtful amulet of a faith healer. Several visits were required, for two weeks, on Tuesdays and Thursdays, if I remember correctly. Each time, the man added some powdery concoction to a large brass bowl that was half filled with water. He chanted mantras and turned the vessel three times around my head—first clockwise and then the other way—before offering it down my body and along my limbs. With each stirring motion, the metal talismans around his neck clinked together like hypnotizing wind chimes.

"Focus," he said. "See how the yellow is being drawn out of your body."

Though Ama was impressed by how orange-yellow the water had become, the magic never cured me.

On one of those endless days, when I lay in bed consumed by weariness and a sense of futility, a glimmer of light appeared. As I reclined against the pillows, I felt the tender touch of someone running their fingers through my hair. "I'm here. Everything is going to be all right," he said. Thatha had returned to my life. My spirits soared, and joy filled my heart.

Thatha had deteriorated in the months since I had last seen him. He appeared older now, wearier, the stress of our separation marked in the lines on his face. I would drift off into a pleasant slumber, and when I awoke, he was still beside me.

"I'll always take care of you," he whispered.

"And I will always take care of you too, Thatha," I said.

Life was wholesome again. Everyone was happy, and even Dad's gambling abated.

Just when life seemed too good to be true, it was indeed too good to be true. A few days after Christmas, in between my grade eleven and twelve years, we received a telephone call. It's never good when the phone rings at 5:30 in the morning. You're not spared, even if you don't have a telephone. Dad took the call at the landlord's house next door. Thatha had passed away.

As we backed out of our driveway, an updraft set a column of air into a violent swirl that collected and scattered trash, leaves, and other debris about. It felt as though Thatha's spirit was beckoning us toward his breathless form.

The undertaker had not yet come to fetch his body, but a rectangular cardboard notice that advertised his funeral was already tied around the lamppost at the intersection of Swan and Lark roads in Duffs Road. Even without reading the notice I could imagine the information that was filled into the blank spaces in between the pre-printed details: Thatha's name boldly inked with a black felt-tipped pen, followed by a procession of immediate relatives, both living and dead. This is how people in the community made the connection necessary to learn who had died.

As I stepped out of the car, I could hear the anguished cries of my aunts. I had shut down all responses, suppressing any outward signs of my own agony. Not even those closest to me would have suspected the intensity of my suffering.

I entered the house of my childhood, trying my best to avoid the intrusive gaze of the neighbors. My aunts were kneeling, distraught, beside his body, with a mourning lament, and calling each of us by name before pronouncing the obvious. At first, I couldn't bear to look directly at his lifeless form, fixing my gaze on Thatha's grey hat that rested undisturbed on its hook. It was in that empty space that the full weight of his absence came over me.

I touched his cold and motionless body, bewildered by the crusted blood around his nostrils, and muted by the intensity of his serenity. Then the tension in my muscles snapped, the internal trembling steadied, and my tears stood still. Even in death, he filled me with a strange sense of calm, like I had been covered in a soft, comforting cloak, reassured that things were going to be all right.

For weeks, I was afraid of the dark, afraid that his image would appear beside my bed, smiling, telling me that he missed me—a ghost without body and soul. Then sadness, shock, disbelief, and even anger, each one, came stacked, one on top of the other. Yet the grief of a teenager is not of the type that is conspicuous in its nature. Despite my rubbery legs, I did not fall to my knees, and the welling up of tears inside me fell inwards and without any hint of sorrow. I needed to be alone, to face my despair in seclusion, without companion and without conversation. My soul wept silently, devoid of any measure of comfort, its heartbreak stretching out through the agony of secretly held pangs: the intense bitterness of our separation; the gloomy misery at the thought of him being absent from my high school and university graduations; the sharp sorrow of him being unable one day to share in my triumph at becoming a doctor, a triumph that held for me the ultimate vindication of all the struggles in his life.

"I'll always take care of you too, Thatha." The weight of regret settled heavily upon me as I realized the missed opportunity to alleviate his agony, to be there for him and provide the care and comfort in his hour of need.

The passing of a parent, regardless of our age or level of preparedness, can trigger a series of responses that compel us to change our course. Despite Thatha's demise, my father's gambling addiction was unaltered. It did not get better, but I'm grateful that it didn't get any worse.

CHAPTER 9

A Crisis of Conscience

Now that Thatha was gone, I felt I had lost my anchor. I was stuck in the doldrums and struggling to find direction in a world offering an uncertain future. What could I do but believe blindly that by some miracle, by some external circumstance, all this would suddenly open out, and a sublime and beautiful vista would rise before me? In my flight into this imaginary world, I could not perceive for myself anything but the best. That is what one thinks about when one has nothing—either to be a hero, or to grovel in the mud. There is nothing in between.

Perhaps subconsciously I was searching for someone to lean on, an emotional proxy of sorts, who would put the wind back in my sails and be the light that would help me navigate the future.

Sometimes we encounter people who begin to interest us at first sight, even before a word is spoken. Our principal at Verulam High School, Mr. M. S. Naidoo, was that kind of person. He was a rigid Latin master, a man of unbending authority, and with a reputation for getting things done.

In Mr. Naidoo's first week at our school, I watched him discipline a student.

"Come here, boy," he said. "What is this I see? This school does not tolerate long hair."

"Uh, I was busy studying this weekend, sir."

"No excuses, boy. You will go home immediately and come back with one of your parents tomorrow. Eight o'clock sharp!"

"But sir…"

"No buts, and don't come back unless those locks are shorn."

Students spoke about him in hushed tones, referring to him as 'Zulu' because he was darker than most of us in our all-Indian school.

Despite his tough exterior, he was a kind and sociable man. It was tennis that made me connect with the silver-haired visionary.

Mr. Naidoo ensured that the school funds, held idly by the chintzy custodians of the past, were mobilized to benefit both the school and the community. He oversaw the construction of tennis courts, and purchased a set of racquets. In a time when school facilities were strictly reserved for students and only accessible during school hours, he opened things up, and actively encouraged community members to play.

My first tennis racquet was a Sunsport, purchased from Game, a store that sold sporting goods, electronics, and clothing. Constructed with a shoddy wooden frame and loose strings, it threatened to fall apart with the very first serve. Despite its poor quality, it was available at a bargain price of five rands (US $5). However, there were only two racquets left, and Poobal and I didn't have enough cash. The following day, we returned with an advance from Ama and retrieved the racquets, which we had carefully concealed beneath a stack of dress shirts.

On weekdays we played tennis for three to four hours at a time, and on weekends even longer. Our opportunity to learn from the world's best tennis coaches was a stroke of luck, made possible only by Ama's good fortune. It was thanks to the Telefunken TV she won in a lucky draw at Asmal's that we were able to mimic the serves and volleys of Bjorn Borg at Wimbledon, the delicate drop-shots of John McEnroe at the US Open, and the topspin lobs of Guillermo Vilas at Roland Garros in Paris.

Every Friday afternoon Mr. Naidoo would join us for a game. Despite being in his sixties he was unusually athletic, and scampered about the court with vigor. I often partnered him in doubles. He was forever eager to improve his game, and was particularly fascinated by the drop-shot. As much as he tried, he held the racquet too stiffly, and tried to hit the ball far too hard.

"Soft hands, Mr. Naidoo," I would say. "Get under the ball and try to absorb the impact. Let it die as it falls over the net."

My flimsy old Sunsport racket carried me to the semifinals of the Coca-Cola High School Championships. I also played in several provincial cricket tournaments, and tried out for volleyball as well. While sports played an important role in my life, it was only the mastery of poetry and prose, algebraic proofs, kinematic graphs, and chromosomal crossovers that had the power to unlock the doors of opportunity.

One Friday afternoon, as we rested in between sets, seeking respite in the shade of tall palm trees, Mr. Naidoo turned to me and posed an unusual question.

"Do you know what *malum in se* means?"

I was caught off guard. Assuming that it was a rhetorical question, I looked at him rather perplexedly.

"It's a Latin phrase that conveys the idea that some things are inherently evil, even if the law deems them to be correct."

This must be important, I thought, especially given that Mr. Naidoo was invoking the power of Latin to convey this principle.

He continued in the style of Churchill's powerful oratory, his voice resonating with conviction, "If we are passive and simply wait for the White schools to extend an invitation, we may wait forever. We must confront them on their sports fields, engage in debates, and assert ourselves in speech contests. Even at the risk of rejection, we must challenge them."

Now that my curiosity had been piqued, I leaned forward, eager to hear more. "What's your plan, Mr. Naidoo?" I asked.

A mischievous glint flickered in his eyes, and there was a hint of daring in his voice. "Let's set our sights on the Jan Hofmeyr Speech Competition," he said.

I had done the elegant math to figure out what it would take to set myself apart from the other competitors. I took every opportunity to participate in speech contests, acted in the school play each year, and became the captain of our school's debating team. We won the Chetty Debating Shield for three consecutive years. Though I was not Muslim, and knew little about Islam, I won the National Arabic Circle Speech Contest after I had substituted for our local team and spoken about the advantages of fasting. I had developed a talent for speaking, an attribute that got me elected as the Youth Mayor of Verulam.

I learned something valuable from each of those experiences, but unlocking my true potential was only possible by transcending the limitations that were imposed upon me. The Jan Hofmeyr contest was the premier provincial competition, but its doors were closed to students of color. To challenge the system in such a bold way was something that I could not resist.

I was not aware of who Mr. Naidoo had negotiated, with and the details of the conversations that were held, but it was agreed that the victor of a runoff 'Indian contest' would be granted the opportunity to participate in the esteemed competition.

My speech, titled "Where there's a Will, there's a Way," earned me the right to represent the North Coast in the finals of the Jan Hofmeyr contest. I felt intimidated, standing before a mainly White audience that night, aware of the hundreds of eyes that would be scrutinizing me, examining every detail of what I had to say. But this was the dance of vulnerability that would ultimately unlock the door of inclusion, so that voices like my own would be heard. I opened my talk by paraphrasing the American poet Henry Wadsworth Longfellow: "Great heights were not achieved by mere flight. While you were asleep, the others worked at night." That got the audience's attention, and I continued with greater confidence. The cases I cited to prove my argument were a testament to the enduring belief that where determination and resilience reside, the doors of possibility swing open. In the end, victory was not mine to have, but the impact of my presence and the power of that presentation paved the way for other students of color to participate in the Jan Hofmeyr contest.

At times it felt as though Mr. Naidoo sat in his office all day, like a magician, dipping into his box of tricks, conjuring provocative spells that could plunder the privilege held by White schools.

So, I was not as surprised when he approached me one day and said, "An Indian girl was accepted into the Rotary Exchange Program last year. Would you like to be the first Indian boy to be selected?"

"What's Rotary, Mr. Naidoo?"

"Rotary does amazing things," he said. "They raise funds for charity, assist underprivileged children, and have a fantastic program that allows high-school students to spend time in a foreign country."

He dangled the possibility of spending an entire year in the United States, Canada, Australia, or New Zealand. What an opportunity, I thought, to connect with students from all over the world, attend an integrated school, and immerse myself in a different culture.

My sights were set on going to medical school in the following year. I was having trouble figuring out how my parents were going to pay for that. Though my hopes were raised, they were blunted by the costs I assumed to be associated with going overseas.

"It's an opportunity of a lifetime," he said.

"I'd love to, but I don't think we can afford that, Mr. Naidoo."

"If you're selected, I promise to raise the money so that you can go."

Given that I had nothing to lose, I was going to do the utmost to be the first boy of color in the Rotary Program.

The first in the series of Rotary interviews was held at the Oyster Box Hotel, a place that held a special place in my heart. Thatha helped build it, and it was the place where he worked until the end.

"It's a grand hotel," Thatha often said.

As a child, I'd longed to visit this forbidden place, the playground of rich White people, perched on a rocky outcrop high above the famous red-and-white lighthouse in Umhlanga Rocks. I relied on my naive imagination to console myself as a child, picturing Thatha bowing devotedly at the appearance of his boss, his grey hat with two big dimples on the crown, pinched delicately between his thumbs and forefingers. "Pardon me, Mrs. Hill…Certainly, Mrs. Hill," he would say and march off to tighten a leaky faucet or knock a nail into a loose piece of siding. After all those years I was finally going to see the Oyster Box.

The night before the interview was spent preparing: practicing facial expressions in front of a mirror, enunciating stock lines in different tones, trying to curate the most favorable presentation. Surely, they would ask about apartheid: what it was like to live in a segregated community, and how it felt to attend an Indian-only school. The issue of race could not be handled in any random manner. It had to be planned out, skillfully and with sensitivity. The rehearsing continued, even through endless fields of sugarcane as we drove to the interview the following afternoon.

I waited my turn, with the clock in the lobby ticking every moment of anxiety. I found myself rocking to the beat of that ticking, pressing my hands into my thighs to control the tremor and the sweating. I focused on the reception staff, trying to humor myself by interpreting their facial expressions in comic ways.

It was not long before I found myself seated before a panel of three adjudicators: two sharply-dressed White men in pinstriped business suits and an Indian man in a white safari suit. They began their interrogation without delay, rifling rapid-fire questions, testing my range, delving into my attitudes, and probing beneath the artificial calm that I projected outwardly.

I maintained a confident posture in defiance of their intrusive gazes, my feet firmly planted and eyes fixed forward with intensity.

While I cannot recall the exact details of the interview, there was one significant moment that remains etched in my memory.

The man in the middle cupped his chin. "By the way, if someone were to ask about your identity, what would you say?"

There was a slyness in that inquiry, an alarm that set about a crisis of countless questions that whizzed about my head. Was he referring to my ancestry? Did he want to know my philosophical perception of self? What was the *real* intention behind his question? For just a moment, I considered using the Buddhist lines, "It's all an illusion. I have no inherent identity." Instead, I started with uneasy hesitation, "I identify as Indian…"

Something flashed beneath the surface of their hardened expressions, and in that instant, I sensed that I was treading on shifting sand. I could see it in the crumpled frown of the one who posed the question, the piercing gaze over the rim of another's glasses, and the gentlest nod of disapproval from the man in doctorly white. How could I retreat towards the safety of firm ground without being swallowed by the quicksand that I found myself in?

But in just a second or two, confidence came over me like lightning igniting a forest fire. I drew myself up, leaned forward in my chair, and completed the sentence with a newfound boldness.

"…but despite the things that define me as Indian, I am most proud to identify as South African!"

The crumpled frown stretched out into a broad beam, his eyebrows arching to the sky. The other nudged his glasses a little higher, as though the rims ought to sit up and pay attention. And the doctorly man smiled, a smile of guarded approval.

I blushed with helpless pride. That was a smart reply and it had come out of nowhere.

The interview left me grappling with conflicting emotions. Did I betray myself by tailoring a response that played into what they wanted to hear? Was it wrong to engage in the acrobatics of cultural code-switching, like a chameleon, sliding unnoticed between worlds, fitting in everywhere and belonging nowhere? As a teenager living in a White-dominated world, I was acutely aware that my identity was confined by borders that I did not create. My life had been inoculated with the idea that I was nothing but Indian. What choice did I have? I pretended to live up to the expectations of the dominant culture so that I would not disqualify myself from the scholarship. It wasn't fair, but it was the only way forward for me.

What does it really mean to be South African, I wondered.

A radio jingle that put a local spin on an American car advert went like this: "We are *braaivleis* (barbecue), rugby, sunny skies, and Chevrolet." But the idea of a collective 'we' had little resonance in South Africa. Some might even argue that the same sun that shone equally on us all cast a different light on everything. There was no shared cultural heritage that bound our people together, no national dish that we could call our own, and no unique culinary tradition that reflected our diverse heritages. While soccer was the most popular sport in the country, it was denied its rightful place on the national stage simply because it was predominantly played by African people. Despite the players' skill and talent, the discriminatory politics of apartheid barred people of color from provincial and national teams.

I waited anxiously, hoping that the springtime breeze that carried the sweet fragrance of jacarandas would bring a favorable response from the Rotary selection committee. The final grade twelve exams were approaching, and the pressure was building. Every day I hurried to the mailbox, quickly flipping through the pile of envelopes, hoping to see the wheel insignia of Rotary International.

Finally, one day, it arrived. My heart raced with a mix of anticipation and trepidation, my fingers trembling. I held my breath as I opened the envelope. I scanned the first paragraph hastily, trying to absorb every word. Then I slowed down and read that paragraph again, making sure that I was not making a mistake. It was a moment of pure disbelief, and, with excitement coursing through my veins, I read the words: "Congratulations! You have been accepted into The Rotary International Student Exchange Program."

It had been an eternity, far too long, since I had experienced such unbridled joy. The vaguely familiar sensation that rose within, that shiver of exaltation, stayed with me for a long time, filling my heart with warmth and elation. I closed my eyes and savored the feeling, allowing it to linger before letting it soak into my bones.

Judge Paul Paulson, the president of the Rotary Club of Youngstown, Ohio, called later that week. He informed me that Youngstown was an industrial city that was in the heart of the steel-producing Rust Belt of America.

"We're still searching for a family that would host you," he said.

I spread out maps on the kitchen table, located Youngstown, and calculated its proximity to more familiar places like New York City and Washington, DC. Even as I performed this small act of tracing out clear lines and computing tangible distances, there was trouble brewing. Protests and boycotts were spreading through Indian high schools in and around Durban.

The years following the Soweto student uprising in 1976 had ushered in a period of intense repression and censorship. Student leaders found themselves either imprisoned or exiled, while a state of emergency gripped the nation. Then, in September of 1980, South Africa once again plunged into turmoil. The community in Soweto rallied against rent hikes, while the armed wing of the ANC, *Umkhonto we Sizwe*, launched grenades at an administrative building in Johannesburg. Simultaneously, explosions reverberated through the Sasol One and Sasol Two chemical plants in the country's interior. Amidst the chaos, Kidar's father, Mr. Ramgobind, and other political activists, were arbitrarily arrested by the police and held without trial.

A wave of student demonstrations broke out across the country. African, Indian, and Coloured (mixed race) high-school students demanded educational opportunities that were equal to their White peers. They boycotted classes in protest. With only a few months left until the end of my high school career, I was hoping for a quiet and uneventful year. However, with widespread dissatisfaction amongst young people in South Africa, it seemed unlikely that our school would escape the tension that was roiling in the rest of the country.

One Monday morning in September of 1980, following assembly, Kidar—who was once again in my class after his family had also moved to Verulam—informed us of the grave situation in high schools around Durban.

"Students have been beaten by the police, and several were arrested," Kidar said. "Some students in Chatsworth have been expelled from school. We must stand together and take control of our education."

Even progressive teachers were hesitant to support our actions. The principal believed that "no good purpose could be served by the boycotts," but he chose to overlook our actions. Despite the risks, we agreed to join the boycott.

My parents did not want me to be part of the boycotts, yet to a teenager the energy of protest is seductive, its danger even exciting. Whilst our teachers oversaw empty classrooms, I joined the rest of the students on the grass banks outside. We chanted slogans: "Equal rights for all" and "Indians will never accept apartheid." However, what I remember most vividly was our agonizing attempts to sing Zulu freedom songs, and how quickly we retreated to the catchy lyrics of Pink Floyd's *Another Brick in the Wall*.

"We don't need no education…Hey, teachers, leave those kids alone!"

These words packed a provocative punch, but more importantly, they rolled off our tongues with ease.

After the initial few days, the fiery speeches and chants that once filled the air were replaced by a sense of weariness and resignation. It felt like the tightropes and trapeze nets were packed away, the bearded lady had already been shaved, and the trumpeting elephants were safely returned to their cages. Our protest, like the once formidable menagerie, was now all hitched up, and the show was over.

On the third day of the boycott, the principal called me into his office. His door stood partially open. I took a deep breath and steadied myself. The principal sat on a haughtily-elevated armchair behind a large oak desk. At first, he said nothing, his eyes resting on the ruby-red badge on my lapel: HEAD PREFECT. He squinted to scrutinize each of the engraved letters before finally speaking.

"Do you know why we chose you?"

His tone was a stark contrast to the friendly chats we'd had after games of tennis on Friday afternoons. I was unsure of how to respond, and gazed out of the window, finding myself staring at my own reflection.

I turned to face him, still unsure of what to say. He stood up, his arms extended like the scales of justice, and he tilted his palms up and down, up and down.

"In times of crisis, we are faced with difficult choices," he said.

Mr. Naidoo came forward and placed his hand on my shoulder. "Think about your parents, and consider those in the community who raised the money for your trip to the USA. What would they say?" Then he went back to his chair, interlocked his fingers, and stared at me expectantly.

Now imagine a teenager, standing on the cusp of scholastic success and, by some cruel twist of fate, cast into a predicament over which he has little control. The stakes are high and the risks great. How that teenager wishes that he did not have to choose between loyalty and self-interest—that it would have been possible to hold onto both. It felt like I had come too far to risk failure now. Expulsion would mean the end of my dreams, not just the Exchange Program, but my entire future, including medical school. I was stuck. What could I do?

How I wished that some sage counsellor could have guided me. I reflected on the wisdom of great heroes such as Gandhi—and Mandela, who was still in prison. What would they have done, given the position I found myself in?

Eventually, I came to the sober realization that I was no Gandhi and no Mandela. It is noble to stand up for the greater good, but that requires insight that comes with age and experience. As difficult as it was, I had to accept that what had seemed brave and laudable only a few days earlier was too much of a risk. I returned to an empty classroom, feeling defeated and ashamed.

I stood alone, feeling as though I had been spat upon. As I watched my peers chatting and laughing, I knew that they must despise me for having let myself sink so low, for having degraded myself so shamelessly. Any false notion of honor and dignity was now gone. I felt cloaked in a silent invisibility.

At one point, as I looked out of the window, a group of students appeared to turn toward me, their hushed whispers sounding more clamorous. In my desperate mind, I imagined explaining myself to them.

"It is not forgiveness that I seek, but only your understanding. If only you could see things from my perspective and appreciate the conflicting thoughts that are racing through my head."

They seemed uninterested in my overtures, and some even looked contemptuously in my direction. All this was disconcerting. The feeling of intense repulsion had by now reached such a pitch that I did not know how to escape this wretchedness.

That evening I was feeling miserable, and tormented by the memories of a challenging few days at school. I had endured disturbing looks that I could not shake off. Other students stared at me.

That night those thoughts spilled over into my dreams. I dreamt about the cherished moments I had spent with Kidar, and how these appeared to be overshadowed by his mocking and spiteful jibes. In my dreams, I tried to remain stoical, and endure his taunts, but I struggled to escape the contempt. All I could envision was him looking down on me with cold and haughty sniggering, and despising me for my selfishness. There was a moment when I woke up with a start, my heart pounding with fear and uncertainty as I struggled to find a way to reconcile my actions with my conscience.

A couple of days later our boycott ended, and the student body resumed classes. However, the weight of scrutiny falls upon those who dare to break ranks first. My deepest desire was to remain loyal, not just to the cause, but also to Kidar and my friends at school—it truly was! Yet, by going against them I unwittingly collided with a fundamental law of the universe. There was no alternative but to bind myself to the dictates of my fate. Though I felt powerless to alter the course of events, it was a price I had to pay.

Kidar, whose father remained in detention, proved to be far from the inconsiderate figure I had assumed in my dreams. Having seen me at my worst, he possessed a depth of understanding that was a great deal more than I had imagined. He grasped the full extent of my predicament, and was still willing to be my friend.

CHAPTER 10

The Social Experiment

With only two weeks left until my scheduled departure, I finally received a message from the folks in Youngstown, Ohio.

"There has been a slight change in plan," said the woman on the other end of the phone. "Unfortunately, we were not able to secure a family that would host you."

A sickening feeling came over me.

"There's good news, though: you're going to Long Island in New York," she continued.

New York! New York! Of all the places in the world, I was going to New York.

My knowledge of New York came mostly from Frank Sinatra's classic song, and movies like *Taxi Driver*. For many days, my mind was consumed by the possibilities of the city that never sleeps. I stayed awake at night, imagining myself ascending to the top of the Empire State Building, watching the sunset from the observation deck of the

World Trade Center, biking in Central Park, circling the Statue of Liberty, and hailing a yellow cab on Fifth Avenue.

I lay awake at night, my mind consumed not only with excitement for my upcoming trip to New York, but also with worries and doubts. Why had no family in Youngstown been willing to host me? Was it the color of my skin that had turned them away? The thought of being rejected based on something beyond my control sent me spiraling into a racial maelstrom filled with anxiety and self-doubt. As I prepared to live with a White family and attend a multiracial school, I couldn't help but wonder how I would be accepted. Would I encounter racism outside the safety of my familiar Indian community? The more I dwelled on these questions, the more I feared the possibility of a miserable year ahead.

I arrived in New York in January of 1981, on the day that coincided with the inauguration of Ronald Reagan as the fortieth President of the United States, and the release of the remaining fifty-two American hostages from captivity in Iran. After trudging into the arrivals hall at JFK, I was confronted by a tackily-mounted poster on the back of the washroom door. The poster, clearly not intended to be part of the décor, had a picture of a bearded man in the crosshairs of a rifle with the words "Put a Holla in the Ayatollah." I was shocked by the graphic detail of the image and the bluntness of its message. It was a stark reminder that I was in America now, a country where political discourse was often polarizing and aggressive.

It was a couple of years prior to the release of the movie *A Christmas Story*, and even if someone had 'triple dog dared' me, I wouldn't have tried to lick a flagpole. Other exchange students had warned me that New York winters were "so terribly cold that an exchange student once got his tongue frozen and stuck on a flagpole." That image was firmly imprinted on my mind, and I was already wearing a body-hugging thermal vest, long-johns, corduroy pants, and a thick flannel shirt.

While waiting to get off the plane I started piling on more layers of clothing, enough to insulate Alaska in winter: a woolen sweater, a fleece-lined jacket, a London Fog trench coat lined with faux fur, woolen mittens, a lambswool scarf, and a balaclava to cover my face.

For a moment, I stood lost in thought, until a porter, trundling along with his luggage trolley, startled me out of my reverie. He appeared to be gazing at some distant horizon when he stopped abruptly, staring at me as if he had just seen the Abominable Snowman. Then he erupted into uncontrollable laughter, doubling over and slapping his thighs in disbelief.

"Bro, there's a heatwave out there," he said, still chuckling.

I was without a doubt embarrassed to have been laughed at in such a way, yet I was struck by how boldly he expressed himself. During my limited interactions with Black people in South Africa, I had not seen such uninhibited behavior. It was refreshing to see a Black person acting with such self-assurance.

I perceived his words to mean, *Hey, take off that balaclava. You're letting down all the people of Africa.* He probably didn't intend to embarrass me, yet I felt as if I had let down the entire African continent. Feeling the weight of my indiscretion, I removed the woolly object of his ridicule and laid bare my shame.

Phew! What a culture shock! This was America, where even Black people acted with unequivocal confidence.

I had spent countless hours picturing that first encounter with my host parents. I hadn't spoken to them or seen their faces, so I couldn't truly anticipate the impact that it would have on me.

A lady with short blonde hair smiled as though I were the best thing she had ever seen, as though she had been waiting for me all her life.

"Hello, Kris," my host mom, Barbara, said in a high, clear voice as she hugged me.

Her husband, Dave Cervone, stood beside her, extending his hand. "Welcome to America. Is it okay if we call you Kris? It sounds very similar to what your mom and dad call you."

I choked with emotion. This was not the way I had imagined it, not for White people to show me that kind of affection.

We journeyed quickly out of the city limits, past huge fluttering American flags, boats anchored in frozen bays, snow-covered farms, and steepled churches with roadside graveyards. Ninety minutes later we arrived in East Marion, near the tip of the North Fork of Long Island.

My new sisters, Michelle, who was sixteen, and Melissa, who was thirteen, welcomed me and led me into the living-room, where the family had gathered. Barbara's mom, Bapcia (Grandma) had brought over some *galumpkis*—steamed cabbage rolls that were stuffed with minced pork and rice. Barbara's dad, Dziadzia (Grandpa) had stayed home.

I settled into a rocking chair, wrapped in a frilly antique quilt that Barbara had made. The walls were adorned with Michelle's life-like artwork, which perfectly captured the beauty of the local beach scenery. A breathtaking three-tiered wedding cake, expertly decorated with white frosting and intricate little roses, sat on the country-style table. Looking back, I regret not taking the time to appreciate fully the amount of effort Michelle had put into crafting those beautiful roses.

"Are you hungry, Kris?" Barbara asked, offering to fix me something to eat.

I found myself in a conundrum, trying to balance politeness and gratitude. It had been several hours since breakfast on the plane, and I wasn't sure what would be an appropriate request. Back home, buttered bread and tea would suffice at any hour, but in New York it might seem out of place. After a moment's hesitation, I decided to go with a safe option.

"If it's not too much trouble, Barbara, I wouldn't mind a burger, please."

"Are you sure, Kris? We can whip up something else if you'd prefer."

Barbara's surprise was evident in her questioning tone, as if my request had caught her off guard. I couldn't help but wonder if she had expected a response more aligned with that of a 'good Hindu boy.'

"I do eat beef, Barbara."

What I hadn't realized was that it was still breakfast time, a time typically reserved for pancakes or waffles in the Cervone household. Adding a lighthearted touch to my first meal with the Cervones, Melissa flashed a sly grin and quipped, "Looks like he's going to eat us out of house and home, Mom."

A few weeks after my arrival, I settled comfortably on the couch with the *Suffolk Times* in my hands. The local newspaper was a delightful change from the political and violent narratives I had grown accustomed to in South Africa. I found the snippets of social gossip particularly amusing:

> "Mrs. Cherry's parents, who had been absent for many years, ventured from Connecticut to pay a visit. They enjoyed a delightful time in East Marion before embarking on their return journey via the Orient Point ferry."

But my humor was short-lived. As soon as I sank into the couch the family cat, Puss, leapt up onto my lap, claiming it as her throne. Each time I tried to get up, her sharp claws sprang into action, locking me in place. The more I tried to pry myself away, the tighter the claw-wielding ninja's grip became. Barbara and Michelle sat back, thoroughly entertained by the comical battle of wills that was playing out before them.

Michelle had to give up her bedroom to me. She was not exactly thrilled with the arrangement, especially since she had to sleep in the basement. Still, she was generous enough to accommodate me. We spent many hours engaged in spirited competition, finding any excuse to prove our superiority. The playful arguments over Battleships, and feuds over memory recall with Simon would intensify, with accusations of cheating frequently thrown around like torpedoes. But there was nothing that infuriated Michelle more than when I ate her marzipan roses.

Michelle had a remarkable artistic flair. Her tiered wedding cakes were a showcase of dramatic design, with each layer clean, crisp, and edged with sugar lace. She crafted delicate roses out of marzipan and set them out on waxed paper in the basement.

I was playing pool in the basement one evening when I noticed a set of iridescent pink roses. I tried my best to resist them, taking care not to look in that direction. I struck another ball into the side pocket and gazed up. There they were again, staring at me enticingly.

"Just one," I told myself. "She wouldn't even notice if one was missing."

One became two, and soon I was in freefall, devouring one sweet dainty after another until they were all gone.

A few days later, I heard Michelle's shrieks from the basement, and I knew that my indiscretion had been uncovered. Michelle was livid. She complained bitterly, and for a whole week, I was given the cold shoulder. Despite it all, Dave and Barbara said nothing to me.

One spring morning, and several weeks after my arrival in East Marion, Dziadzia finally came over to meet me. He was dressed in his work clothes: steel-toed boots, bibbed overalls, and with a wrench sticking out of his pocket. Over the last forty years he had run a one-man plumbing operation out of his old Dodge van that was stocked with adjustable wrenches, plungers, tube cutters, and pipes of all shapes and sizes.

At first, he avoided direct eye-contact with me, introducing himself softly, his words carrying a gentle timidity that mirrored his reserved nature.

"I need to replace a faulty water tank," he said. "Would you like to help me?"

I had no experience with plumbing, but I agreed anyhow.

We were cramped together in the narrow confines of a stranger's utility room, bent over as if in prayer, with our souls seemingly on hands and knees, when Dziadzia chose to perform the emotional equivalent of the Heimlich maneuver. Something had been choking him for weeks, and he chose this moment to finally cough it up.

"Kris, I've had some tough moments in my past. Sometimes we think bad things about others, and sometimes others think badly of us," he said.

There was a look of unease on his face, and I wondered where this meditative sentiment was leading.

"In my native Poland, I hardly ever saw people with dark skin like yours," he said. "We called them colored folk. They were not like us, and we could not trust people who were not like us. I know it's wrong, Kris, but that's how I grew up."

I saw an imploring sense of regret and pain in his steel-blue eyes.

"At first I thought Barbara and Dave were crazy, but now I have changed. I'm happy you're with us, Kris."

By Easter, I was comfortably settled into my new life with the Cervones in East Marion. I was excited to be involved in the preparations for a traditional Polish celebration. I quickly learned that liking eggs was key to enjoying Polish Easter. For dinner that night we were having *Sledz*, which consisted of gutted and filleted herring, soaked in vinegar and served with boiled eggs sliced into quarters, and *Zurek*, a soup soured with fermented rye, and garnished with hard-boiled egg halves.

On Easter Saturday the girls and I were seated at the kitchen table creating *pisanki*—white hard-boiled eggs decorated with colorful designs, that would eventually become the objects of a real Easter-egg hunt. I was splotching down another lustrous pink polka-dot when the back of my hand caught my attention.

I noticed the contrast in the color of our hands. My hands were undeniably brown, and the intensity of their darkness dawned upon me gradually, and then suddenly. I became startled, convinced that this was not my skin, that somehow it did not belong to my body. I stared abjectly, wondering if the light was playing some nasty trick.

Eventually, I turned my hands over to the lighter, more agreeable side, as though I were conferring a favor upon those around me. Yet no one else in the room was the least bit bothered by the color of my skin.

My entire life had been lived in a society of the same exclusive Brownness. Brown family, Brown neighbors, Brown friends, Brown teachers, even Brown doctors. I existed in a kind of conditioned oblivion, melting like cocoa into a chocolate cake. Then, in an unsuspecting moment, and for no good reason, I came to believe that I was darker than I had assumed.

At the dinner-table that evening, home in South Africa felt like a distant memory. As I looked across at my new family and the plates piled high with food, laughter filling the air, I felt secure in the idea that I was surrounded by people who loved me, and that I truly belonged. Earlier in the day I had been overly self-conscious about the color of my skin; but now I realized that there was no need for an emergency infusion of skin-lightener. The Cervones accepted me just the way I was, and they loved me as though I had always been a part of their family. Who would have thought that I would feel such a sense of belonging in a White family?

At the start of each school morning at Greenport High School my classmates and I would rise and recite the Pledge of Allegiance to the American flag. However, in April, The Dude asked, "Why would a South African pledge allegiance to the flag of the United States?"

I'm not sure how he acquired the nickname 'The Dude,' but whenever someone addressed our social studies teacher, Mr. Manwaring, as The Dude, it brought a smile to his face and put a bounce in his step. Every stride he took seemed to carry a touch of whimsy, as if he were dancing to a rhythm that only he could hear. Behind his thick, round spectacles, there was a glint of wisdom mixed with a hint of unpredictability.

A few days earlier I had shared a story about how torn I felt when I was asked to sing the South African national anthem at a recent Rotary convention. The Dude fidgeted and rolled his head as I recounted that experience.

During the spring break in 1981, the Rotary District of Long Island held a conference at the Castle Harbour Hotel in Bermuda. All twenty-seven exchange students, from sixteen different countries, were flown there on Eastern Airlines.

At the final night's gala event, I strutted around in my official Rotary jacket. It was adorned with lapel-pins I had exchanged for the golden springbok buttons I brought from South Africa. The pins included clogs from Holland, an official badge from the 1980 Moscow Olympics, a voodoo doll from Brazil, the wings of a US pilot who had been shot down over Japan during World War II, and a tomahawk from a steakhouse. The last item, a wisecrack memento, was the result of my repeatedly sending back my steak until it was well done—'killed,' as they put it.

The initial pride I felt in my Rotary jacket quickly disappeared when the students were asked to band together in their national groups and present a song or dance from their home country. While the band played Boney M's *Brown Girl in the Rain*, I realized that I could do no better than tap my toes to the beat. My knowledge of songs was limited to the Afrikaans ballads that were forced upon us in primary school.

Renata, one of the exchange students from Brazil, tried to convince me to perform traditional African drumming. She had heard the Afro-Brazilian rhythms back home and was curious as to whether that sounded like real African drumming. For a moment, I considered the catchy drumbeat of *Ipi Tombi*, a story about a young tribesman leaving his wife and village to work in the gold mines of South Africa. I had no confidence in my ability to improvise. My lack of talent would be too apparent.

I looked at Heather, the other exchange student from South Africa, hoping that she would come up with something. Heather was White and spoke Afrikaans, and although we didn't have much in common, we had become close friends over the last few months. She came up with the bright idea of singing the national anthem, *Die Stem*.

"Everyone in South Africa knows *Die Stem*," she said.

The tropical heat had settled, but a deep sense of panic took root in me. There was no longer any joy in the music of *Brown Girl in the Rain*. I was familiar with *Die Stem*. After all, I was forced to sing it at all the official primary school events. Singing *Die Stem* would be too much of a betrayal: yet what else could I do?

Then a spark came over me. "Let's sing *Suikerbossie ek wil jou hê* ('Sugarbush, I Want You So')" I said to Heather. Imagine her shock, her utter astonishment that I even knew that ballad.

I stopped pledging allegiance to the flag on the day The Dude questioned me about it. On the same day, in the social studies class, we watched an episode of Alex Haley's classic, *Roots*. At the time the miniseries was an inescapable and undeniable topic of conversation. The Dude was captivated by Kunta Kinte's struggle to maintain his African identity.

The Dude had this outrageous notion that I should have an opinion on all things related to the vast continent of Africa. In the minds of my classmates, too, Africa was a place filled with mud huts, starving children, streets overrun by lions, and a language that they liked to call 'African.'

"Does apartheid make it difficult for you to identify with Africa, Kris?" Mr. Manwaring asked.

"Unlike Kunta Kinte, my struggle is not one of identity, but of belonging," I said.

"How so?"

"Well, apartheid separates us by race, and each group lives in its own silo. This has allowed me to connect deeply with Indian culture and traditions, but I don't have a larger, national experience to connect with. I don't feel like I belong in South Africa."

For a moment, The Dude was awed into an extraordinarily meditative silence.

"That's why I have difficulty singing our national anthem. I just can't feel patriotic about it," I added.

"But you have no problem pledging allegiance to the flag of the United States," he said as he paced back and forth.

I wasn't sure if The Dude was asking rhetorically or if he wanted a response.

"At first, I believed the pledge was like the Lord's Prayer. I honestly did," I said.

Prone to flights of fancy, The Dude often veered off topic, fixating on something that had caught his attention, and running with it. Now he put one foot on his chair, placed the tip of one arm of his glasses in his mouth, and muttered like a confused old man, "The Lord's Prayer, the Lord's Prayer…"

"I wanted to feel included, like I was part of that larger experience," I continued. "I thought it would be rude not to join my classmates in making the pledge."

The lunch bell rang, but The Dude didn't seem to hear it. He remained in a catatonic pose, repeating, "The Lord's Prayer, the Lord's Prayer…"

There was no official segregation, but during the lunchbreaks White kids sat with White kids and African-American kids with African-American kids. I was at first surprised by this pattern of segregation that mirrored the neighborhood geography. I had not expected this, but the minority African-American community was concentrated in a small, underserved area of Greenport.

As I sat at a table with Michelle and her White girlfriends, happily munching on my peanut butter and jelly sandwich, I noticed some of the African-American kids giving me a look that was more befitting a jilted lover. It bothered me that I had very little interaction with them, and I couldn't help but feel the strain of the physical and social distance between us.

I remember the first time I met Jerome. It was in social studies class.

"Are you taking mathematics?" I asked.

"Hold up, where you from? You talkin' like you straight outta Buckingham Palace or somethin'."

Whatever it was, some of the African-American kids felt that the wrong voice was coming out of my face. Someone who looked much like they did ought to have sounded more like them. My voice, devoid of Serengeti-scented, drum-beating vibrancy, disrupted their romanticism around indigenous languages.

I began to wonder whether there is such a thing as a Black voice, or a White voice, or a Brown voice. It troubled me that my manner of speaking, the subtle ways in which I embellished a sentence or emphasized a point, might create a further disconnect between us. For a time, I became vigilant about the way I spoke, trying my best to ferret out any nuances of accent that they might have considered distasteful. But there were other African-American kids who were charmed by the articulate way I spoke English.

"Kris is a prince from Africa. That is why he speaks the Queen's English," I overheard someone say. My manner of speaking must have been the product of royal grooming.

Whether I had the 'wrong' voice or a 'princely' voice of status—either way—the way I sounded muddled the sense of connection between me and the African-American kids. Like Kunta Kinte, we too were immigrants straddling different cultures, each struggling to find that balance between identity and assimilation.

The relationship between us was complex, a tug-of-war between how we saw ourselves and who we really were. Our experiences with racism, colonialism, and slavery were dissimilar, and our sensitivities to these issues evolved in ways that made it tricky for us to relate to each other. I came to understand that assimilation was a race toward a horizon that was not fixed. The ideal was ever shifting, and my accent would never be perfect.

Watching a marathon of Black television shows like *Good Times*, *The Jeffersons*, and *Sanford and Son*, or cheering Reggie Jackson when he hit a homer for the Yankees, did not help to bridge that divide. Therefore I jumped at the opportunity when Jerome invited me to supper in Greenport.

The play area where I met Jerome had the ruined look of a forgotten summer. The basketball court was a patch of cracked concrete, overrun in places by weeds and sprigs of tall grass. It lay right beside abandoned railway tracks, alongside rusted carcasses of broken cars, vacant lots, the cemetery, and rows of dilapidated houses. The fence that once ran round the perimeter was uprooted, and lay amongst candy-wrappers trodden into the dead leaves.

I went through the line of familiar high-fives, flipping my hands over in response to "And on the Black side, man." Jerome tried his best to teach me the moves, but despite his efforts, I just couldn't seem to get it right. After my second failed attempt at making a basket, the boys erupted into a fit of giggling.

Jerome demonstrated the perfect jump shot, rising up over a defender and expertly knocking down the shot through the rim.

"It comes so naturally for you, Jerome, like Kareem Abdul-Jabbar," I said.

'It ain't 'cause I'm Black, man. We put in a whole lotta practice."

The seemingly innocent was not innocent at all. Both Jerome and I felt the emotional shift and wanted to get past it as quickly as possible.

Jerome's mom, Mrs. Porter, was waiting for us at the door and she broke into a wide-eyed smile as we entered. I was not sure how to greet her, but without hesitation she gathered me into a warm embrace.

Mrs. Porter was a slight, vibrant-looking woman, with silvery hair that peeped out from under her floral *dhuku*. Having grown up in the segregated American South, she exuded a sense of grace and resilience that belied the challenges she had undoubtedly faced.

Soon after our arrival, Mrs. Porter announced, "Dinner is all set. Let's go to the kitchen."

Their home reminded me of our house in Verulam. It was one of those old, run-down, peeling places that smelt like mold inside. The floors creaked beneath the linoleum, and the faucet, stained green from oxidation, dripped incessantly above the kitchen sink. There was no central heating. In the winter, dampness must surely seep through the cracks in the windowpanes.

Mrs. Porter placed a generous slice of cornbread beside my bowl of lentil soup. We spoke as we ate, our conversation gradually drifting towards Africa, as was common whenever I had discussions with Americans.

"Tell me, Kris, are Black folks still mistreated in Africa?" Mrs. Porter asked, her brow furrowed with concern.

"I think Black people in America are treated better than how African people are treated in South Africa," I said. Mrs. Porter listened intently, her eyes filled with sadness and empathy.

"Why does the color of our skin gotta be the reason for all this anger, hate, and pain?" Then Mrs. Porter's head sank. "Kris, it ain't much better for us here. They label us as welfare recipients, saying we don't care 'bout our homes, callin' 'em 'negro huts' and blamin' us for messin' up the neighborhood. But it ain't like that. We barely got enough to make ends meet. Every time I go to the store, I'm shocked at the crazy prices they slap on food and clothes."

"I'm so sorry to hear that, Mrs. Porter."

"It ain't 'bout who's right or wrong. It's 'bout this messed-up system we livin' in. It ain't 'bout good intentions or bad intentions. It's an unjust system, plain and simple."

Mrs. Porter's eyes lit up. "Mandela," she said. "He still locked up?"

It was heartwarming to witness the central place that Nelson Mandela held in the hearts of African Americans. They would almost always ask about Mandela, their words infused with a sense of longing, as one would inquire about a long-lost relative.

Mrs. Porter's words echoed what I had encountered a few weeks earlier on the 7-train to Times Square. As the train screeched around a corner, the car lurched abruptly to the left, and two African-American men burst through the doors of the coach in front.

"Yo, where you from, bro?" they asked.

Just the mention of South Africa sent them into a rapturous ecstasy. "Maandela! Maandela!" they hailed, and I received two simultaneous high-fives and "on the Black side as well."

When it was time to bid farewell to Dave and Barbara at JFK, I knew that they would always hold a special place in my heart, and that they would forever be my Mom and Dad in America. My White family taught me the importance of empathy and forgiveness. I discovered that lengthy sermons on discrimination are less effective in changing attitudes than establishing genuine connections and allowing people the space to empathize and understand one another.

I also came to realize that navigating racial boundaries is fraught with difficulty. Mrs. Porter's poignant appeal for justice reminded me of the pledge of allegiance and the social studies class I had taken with The Dude. I had witnessed the loyalty with which African-American and White students swore allegiance to the flag. Yet I question the implausibility of justice framed in an earnest pledge. The freedom that it espoused was marred by the unbounded promise—yet hypocrisy—that it carried. I had associated racism with the explicitness of apartheid, but failed to see the more subtle signs: how we inadvertently stereotype people based on their race, and how the geography of racism creates physical spaces that define what is possible in people's lives.

CHAPTER 11

My Textbook of Learning

While I was in New York a few Rotarians from Suffolk County arranged an interview at Stony Brook University. I was offered a full scholarship to study medicine. My parents would have no part in that. They wanted me back home.

"I agreed to just one year," Ama said.

In anticipation of my acceptance into medical school, my family had already moved from Verulam to Effingham Heights, a suburb of Durban. I did not raise too much of a protest, as I was not mentally prepared for another six years in America.

In October of 1981, while I was still in New York, I submitted my application to the University of Natal Medical School. Among the approximately eleven medical schools in South Africa, this was the only institution accessible to people of color. The wait for a response felt endless, lasting as long as an elephant's pregnancy. It was not until a week after my return to South Africa, in mid-January of 1982, and just a week before the commencement of lectures, that I finally received a reply.

If Stony Brook deemed me worthy, then perhaps I had done enough to secure a place in medical school in South Africa. There was no guarantee that I would be accepted, given the fierce competition for the one hundred spots that were available. Yet that reckless self-confidence prevented me from making any backup plans.

My emotions upon learning that I was successful, that I was finally to start this journey towards a lifelong ambition, were somewhat muted. They were far short of the ecstasy that I had experienced after being selected for the Exchange Program. I suppose there's a truth to the notion that success breeds success, but that as one becomes more successful, the emotional impact tends to diminish.

The first year of the six-year program was at the Wentworth Campus of the University of Natal, Black Section—UNB. The campus, on Tara Road, was fifteen kilometers from the main teaching faculty at King Edward VIII Hospital, and located in an area that was zoned for 'Coloured' (mixed race) people.

After a 6 a.m. start and an hour and a half's journey on two buses, I was greeted by an abandoned military barracks that was to be my place of learning for the following year. The buildings were derelict and grime-grey, tainted by the kerosene trails of low-flying jets approaching the nearby Louis Botha Airport, and the suffocating fumes from the Mobil oil-refinery next door. I embraced this environment (that had once served to transform the individual pursuits of White boys into a collective military will) as my personal bootcamp, a transformative rite of passage that would shape my transition from adolescence to manhood.

For the first time in South Africa I was in a mixed class, with African, Indian, and Coloured students. After my year in America I felt more comfortable with White teachers, but I still had to adjust to their new teaching styles. There was the free-spirited physics guy who had an uncanny knack for defying convention. He arrived in class wearing shorts, a T-shirt, and sandals. Like a juggler performing for a street audience, he would pull out an old tennis ball, let it fall to the ground and bounce along.

"Now draw out the acceleration-time curve," he would say.

There was also the traditional English gentleman who spoke in short sentences with long pauses, and elaborated breeding experiments by way of a punnet square. Then there were those lecturers with whom it was impossible to get comfortable.

Mr. Paris was a highly-strung man with clipped silvery hair and a stark blue gaze. His racist attitudes created our climate, his mood our daily weather. He wielded such power that on a given day his sarcastic laugh might have been the extent of our joy, his incessant mocking our constant misery.

Mr. Paris had the habit of prancing about in his white lab coat, like a warden stalking maximum-security prisoners. Whenever he was close by, it felt as though I could sense the warmth of his breath on the back of my neck. During one lab session, my partner, an African student, was particularly nervous, as he had never been in a laboratory before. His eyes were wide, and his fingers quivered as he struggled to deliver a precise aliquot of distilled water from beaker to measuring cylinder. Sweat rolled off his shiny forehead and threatened, at any moment, to fall into the mixture and alter its concentration. Mr. Paris's face turned a luminous pink and with a voice holding just a shade of venom, he said, "If this is the cream of the crop, then I shudder to think what the scum looks like."

Wentworth was an avoidable inconvenience. First-year medical students could easily have been accommodated at the main university campus at Howard College. The medical school and the King Edward VIII Hospital, where we completed years two to six, were located just down the road from Howard College.

In contrast to the facilities in Wentworth, Howard College boasted fifty acres of pristine real estate, offering sweeping views of the city of Durban, its harbor, and the Indian Ocean in the distance. Its lecture halls were state-of-the-art, its laboratories well equipped, and its sports fields among the finest in the country. I wish I could tell you that this was my campus, that I played on the grass pitch at Hammond Field Cricket Oval, but non-Whites were not allowed to attend this part of the University.

While my first year was an adjustment to people and their different styles, the subsequent years at the main teaching facility were an exposure to death, disease, and the suffering of Black people in South Africa.

When I was a second-year student, the instantly recognizable smell of formaldehyde trailed me everywhere, and announced my presence well ahead of my arrival. I knew that this odor was my odor, soaked deep into my skin, but for the life of me I was unable to smell it.

Professor Kane had a Renaissance mastery of anatomical drawings. He had just sketched colorful chalk impressions of the anatomical structures that we were to dissect. As I was waiting in the cafeteria, visualizing the relations of the muscles and tendons, I realized how that whiff of formaldehyde had the power to disperse an entire table of people. Even when I walked towards the dissecting hall, senior students smiled and darted away from my path.

In the basement, where the dissecting hall was located, twenty-five Black corpses lay unwrapped, and arranged in orderly rows, on cold steel gurneys. I stood over my cadaver and took a moment to reflect on the substance of what lay before me. I touched the body that was now permanently robbed of its warmth. It was a sobering reminder of the cold reality of death. The poverty of her ribs, her pale tongue and stiffened shoulders were grim reminders of the heavy burdens she must have carried in her life. Her eyes remained half open, as though she was looking out for relatives who might yet come from the rural homelands and claim her.

Dr. Berjak, our anatomy lecturer, walked slowly down the rows, bent over in a stooped position, and with his hands clasped behind his back. He stopped beside a model of a human skeleton, under a mist of formaldehyde—a collective three decades' worth—that hung in the air like an invisible cloud.

"The spirit of the dead bears constant witness to our actions," he said.

It felt so eerie to hear an old White man confer in death a dignity that had probably never been afforded them in life.

I raised my scalpel, the surgeon in me stirring with excitement. Then I paused, filled with indecision, and hesitant to make that first cut. My stomach churned and my hands trembled. Soon the exposed muscles, tendons, and a network of arteries and veins stood bare and undifferentiated. The picture appeared more like Professor Kane's illustrations, less human, and therefore more agreeable.

Under the scrutiny of my blade, the dead became eloquent. The heart that once throbbed, the brain that sensed, and the blood that coursed through those veins protested an identity with the rest of humankind. The anatomy, once stripped of its dark gift-wrapping, gave no clue about belonging to a White person, or a Black person, or a Coloured person, or an Indian person.

The clinical part of my training, in years four to six, was at The King Edward VIII Hospital, a major provincial facility, deposited awkwardly between the White residential area of Umbilo and the coal-powered smokestacks of Congella. Although the hospital was designated for non-White patients, it primarily served the African population. White doctors were permitted to practice and teach at King Edward, as it was the center of medical academia. However the nursing staff was entirely composed of Black individuals, as the few White matrons had opted out of their positions years ago rather than being subjected to taking orders from non-White doctors.

If it was in death that I saw our common humanity, then it was in the living that I came to see the suffering that apartheid imposed upon the most vulnerable amongst us. I realized that disease did not come coded with racially-colored tags, or barcodes based on class. It struck indiscriminately, and was offered at a huge discount to those made more destitute by avoidable social and economic factors.

For years I had dreamt about my first encounter with patients: about all those ailing souls who were waiting, waiting for *me* to come and unravel their complicated illnesses. I dreamt too that I was furiously jotting down notes, listening to chests, looking into mouths, and palpating patients' tummies. Oh, and in those dreams, how smart I appeared, in formal pants with collared shirt and tie, a crisp white lab coat, and a stethoscope wrapped proudly around my neck.

I passed by Hut 4 as I made my way towards D Ward. Hut 4 was one of four wooden structures raised on stilts. It resembled a long Rainbow chicken barn rather than a hospital ward. A prowling cat leapt out from under the hut, darting across as though it was pursuing a mouse. It was never an exaggeration to assume that the cat's scurrying would be rewarded.

D Ward was a newer brick building, filled with rows of beds that overflowed with patients admitted during the previous night. There were patients scattered about, lying on thin mattresses on a cold and unforgiving floor. An elderly man, gaunt and wasted from tuberculosis, lay in a bed, coughing up blood from the caverns that the disease had excavated in his lungs. Curled up on the floor nearby, a teenaged boy lay in a state of stupor, his gaze, dull and distant, mirroring the characteristic obtunded look that accompanied typhoid fever. Next to him was a middle-aged lady, shivering with the fevers of malaria that came like clockwork every two days. Each patient was like a chapter in a medical textbook, brimming with invaluable lessons that could enliven any student's passion for medicine.

The doctors were busy doing rounds when I arrived that morning. One of the interns, a cocky young chap, approached me.

"You should examine the young girl in bed 12. She has a very interesting murmur," he said.

"That sounds good. We just studied the characteristic sounds of heart murmurs," I said.

"This would not be one you would have seen in a textbook," he said.

"That sounds interesting," I said.

"You know how Professor Seedat likes to describe stuff in fancy ways. He calls this murmur 'Bubbling Bumblebeats.'"

"Bubbling Bumblebeats, really?" I said.

"He'll be impressed if you describe it in that way."

I found my patient lying passively in bed, a vision of quiet suffering, with beseeching eyes that beckoned some skilled person to come and give her relief.

"*Unjani*," I said. At first she did not reply to my enquiry about how she was feeling. She slowly raised her gaze and responded in a soft, almost inaudible voice.

"*Kulungile*," she said, indicating that she was all right.

I was so excited to hear the murmur that I forgot to ask any further questions. I slid the diaphragm of my stethoscope beneath her left breast and listened with intensity, first over her heart and then to both lungs. With the idea of 'bubbling bumblebeats' firmly deposited in my head, the whooshes and swooshes I heard did sound very much like the rhythmic fluttering of a bee's wings. And yes, this was a condition unlike any I had encountered in my handbook of signs and symptoms.

Unbeknownst to me, I had fallen into the clutches of a mischievous bunch. The registrars and interns stood waiting for the start of rounds as though they were lying in ambush, relishing the prospect of a newbie making a fool of himself.

The consultant, Professor Y. K. Seedat, was a legendary practitioner, an astute clinician with a titanic personality. He had a sharp dress-sense, wore gold-rimmed glasses, and had short, greying hair. He must have spent countless hours honing the skill of pattern recognition, as he was able to rattle off long lists of signs and symptoms, causes and consequences. He had an uncommon gift for reassurance, making his patients feel that he understood their situation, registered their suffering, and was really listening to them.

"Who will present this case?" the professor asked.

I stepped forward.

"The young girl has rheumatic fever. It licks the joints and bites the heart," Professor Seedat said.

Hearing his eloquent aphorism, primed with a canine twist, reassured me about the possibility of 'bubbling Bumblebeats.'

The Professor adopted a genial, almost good-tempered air as he sat on the bed beside the young girl. He set down the clipboard-chart and took her hand, before addressing me.

"How did this young lady develop rheumatic heart disease?"

I had no idea about the circumstances which led to her illness. The murmur was all I focused on. "She has a murmur related to rheumatic fever. It sounded like bubbling bumblebeats," I said.

"Bubbling bumblebeats? That's hilarious," said the professor.

I was totally crushed, a bungling idiot who had not disappointed the comical ideas that had arisen in the minds of the registrars and interns. A humiliated smile strayed across my lips, my hands trembled, and a rush of panic raced through my mind as I faced the professor.

"You have made a common mistake. It is not unusual for novice students to see patients as entities of disease rather than people."

The professor turned toward the group. "We need to step out of the narrow confines of our world, and for just a moment walk in the shoes of this young lady. Consider what it must feel like for this child, and for her family."

He paused for a moment before continuing.

"Be a good listener. Listen. Listen to the patient. Ask the right questions, then sit back and listen again."

If I had taken the time to explore, to *listen*, then I would have understood more clearly how everyday life had impacted the course of her illness: I would have learnt that she lived in a mud hut that was shared with her parents and five siblings, and that she drank water from a river, the same river where they washed their clothes, and in which the animals waded to cool off from the afternoon heat. I would have realized that they had no money to afford the bus-fare to the clinic, and that the young girl, with a raging fever and sore throat, was too weak to walk the hour-long route along dusty, winding trails to the clinic. And even if her joints had somehow allowed her to get there that Wednesday, the clinic would have been closed, because it was only open on Tuesdays and Thursdays; and even if it was a day when the clinic was open, the penicillin that cost pennies, that could have treated her strep throat and prevented this complication, was out of stock.

That afternoon I signed up for the journey. I understood that I would have to *listen* in a whole new way. I listened, even to those who remained silent, who raised no protest, not a moan, not a groan, not a sound. I listened to the child with malnutrition who lay motionless in his cot bed, too weak to ward off the flies that hovered undisturbed over his open mouth and used his face as a landing pad. I listened to a little girl who had an intravenous catheter placed on her scalp because her limbs were too swollen from the lack of protein. I listened to and watched a three-year-old crawling along the linoleum floor, the belt of his blue bathrobe dragging behind him. In the midst of such despair, it became clear how the diseases of hunger had robbed these children not only of their bodies, but of their spirits as well.

September and October were the months in which the obstetric wards experienced a surge of patients. Women in labor found themselves alone, in an undignified row, five or six patients side by side, their feet up in stirrups and knees spread apart, breathing heavily, screaming, bearing down, and pushing. All the while, they remained exposed, like cattle, and at the mercy of multiple examinations by doctors, nurses, and medical students. Their partners were six hundred kilometers away and three kilometers underground, working in the gold mines of Johannesburg. The *dompass* laws prohibited the women from living close to their partners. The men came home once a year, at Christmas time, and nine months later the women delivered alone, in this factory-like production line.

I tried to do the impossible, to *listen* to the women who were close to delivery, but they would have none of that: "*Akhipe ingane. Akhipe ingane,*" just get the baby out, they screamed.

A medical student's work is never done. There were journal articles to review, tutorials to attend, patients to clerk, blood to be drawn and walked over to the laboratory, medications to be ordered, and biopsies to be performed. In all that chaos, everything other than the most pressing concerns tends to be overlooked. Yet my time on the wards was not always filled with death and despair.

I was in my element in the cafeteria one morning, elaborating the causes of jaundice to a small group of medical students. That was quite the sketch I had drawn: of the liver, bile ducts, and gallbladder, with the head of the pancreas embraced in the "C" of the duodenum. I took my gaze off the drawing and espied a young lady who was watching me intently, but not really listening.

You just know when someone is looking at you that way. I saw it in the galaxies that shone back, in the delicate way she teased a lock that had fallen out of place, and the coyness with which she folded her arms across her breasts. I saw all of these things because I, too, heard the whisper of soft melodies in the wind, and my heart raced as though it was serenading the throbbing glow of a full moon in the night sky.

I was distracted now, unsure about what I said in the rest of that tutorial. I found myself seeking her out, eager to strike up a conversation.

"There is an interesting patient on the ward," I said. I addressed the entire group, avoiding the impropriety, the obviousness of inviting her alone.

The following morning I was filled with excited energy, buoyed by the prospect of seeing Adashnee again. She was dressed like an angel, in a flowing white cotton dress, with a sparkle in her eyes, and her hair set for a special occasion. I rejoiced to the extent of being downright dazed.

My patient was a young boy who had a raging fever, accompanied by a headache and a stiff neck. It sounded like meningitis and needed to be confirmed by a lumbar puncture. The boy looked helpless and anxious, but surrendered himself to the mercy of my self-flattery without the slightest complaint.

I masked and put on my gloves, speaking deliberately, promising to explain each step to the group. With the child sitting up on the edge of the bed, I cleaned the area over his lower spine, threaded a fine needle into the space between the two vertebrae, and carefully collected the spinal fluid into vials.

After the procedure I stood up confidently, but my damsel looked pale and about to crumple into a heap. Was it fate or mere circumstance? Perhaps I'll never know, but this was like the fleeting sunrise, and if I had waited too long, I would have missed it completely. And so it was that I gathered Adashnee into my arms, knowing that, as unlikely as it was, I had found love in the wards of King Edward VIII Hospital.

The early stages of my medical training endowed me with a greater understanding of the human condition. I was granted a deeper wisdom, one that elevated my perception of myself and the world around me. This enlightenment brought forth a profound realization, a realization that I had unearthed my true calling in life. This yearning that had been swarming inside me all this time finally found an outlet, and I began to comprehend the surge of warmth and excitement that enveloped me whenever I helped those in need. Finding love made everything all the more worthwhile. These experiences fostered a stronger connection to the land of my birth, and I discovered a newfound sense of belonging.

CHAPTER 12

A Complicated Relationship

My time in New York gave me a sense of renewed hope that it was indeed possible for people from different racial backgrounds to coexist in harmony in a multiracial society. New York was different, because I immersed myself in a pre-established world with pre-existing social norms. Life carried on as usual around me: I only had to conform to my new environment.

Back in South Africa I found myself at the center of a significant change. For the first time in our lives, African, Indian, and Coloured students were brought together in a single school. This presented a unique opportunity to break free from the barriers that had long divided us, and an extraordinary chance to foster unity.

Yet our relationships struggled to find a clear definition. We conversed in generalities, engaged in trivial discussions, and were hesitant to breach the emotional fortifications that separated us. Sensitive topics were avoided altogether, or approached with caution as though we were treading upon a precarious wooden footbridge that spanned the vast expanse of the Grand Canyon. We were reluctant to discuss the intimate details of our lives, our hopes and fears, and perhaps our suspicions of one another, lest such spontaneous utterances send us plummeting to the depths of the canyon floor.

During meal breaks and in tutorial groups we sat in racially-segregated clusters, Indian students with other Indian students, and African students with their African peers. I stood shoulder to shoulder with my African colleagues, joined them in the chorus of Zulu freedom songs, yet I was oblivious to the substance of their daily struggles and the profound significance behind those melodic verses. When the day ended and I left the hospital, I retreated to the familiar embrace of a working-class Indian community.

During our community health rotation in March or April of 1984, my clinical partner Billy and I were driving towards the cloud-engulfed mountain that gave Montebello Hospital its name. During the first thirty minutes of the two-hour journey we struggled to make any meaningful conversation. Each attempt to start a dialogue ended in an uncomfortable silence that left us both yearning for a connection.

Once we had passed Tongaat, the road twisted and ascended sharply as we veered away from the highway. Dirt paths branched off into a seemingly infinite forest of blue-gum trees, their tall forms concealed by rolling blankets of fog. I glanced at Billy, and in that misty moment I realized how little I knew about him or any of my other African colleagues at medical school.

"Billy…Billy," I said. "I've been thinking. We've attended lectures, worked on laboratory experiments, and found ourselves in the same tutorial groups, yet I feel like I hardly know you."

"It's not an easy journey," he said. "We're still battling to shrug off the divisions that apartheid has imposed on us."

"Where is home for you, Billy?"

A nostalgic smile curved his lips.

"I hail from Ha-Ramakgopa," he said. "It's in the Lebowa 'Bantustan', in the far Northern Limpopo Province of South Africa. Ha-Ramakgopa means 'the place or village of the Ramakgopa clan.'"

"That's remarkable! Your name and your village share the same identity."

"It takes a village for African people to raise a child, you know." His eyes sparkled with mischief.

I chuckled. That's quite a cool response, I thought.

"I am from the Batlôkwa tribe that descends from Queen Manthatise and her son Chief Sekonyela."

"Chief Sekonyela! *The* Chief Sekonyela!" I was excited to be in the presence of someone who traced their bloodline all the way back to Chief Sekonyela, the very figure from our history lessons, from whom Piet Retief had recovered Dingane's stolen cattle.

"People think that all Black people share the same background," Billy said. His voice carried a hint of somberness now. "African students, like me, come from diverse tribes, each with its own unique history."

I remained captivated, hungover from the intoxication of stumbling upon this significant historical connection. The notion of how easily we tend to lump people who appear different from us into a shapeless, formless mass also crossed my mind, yet I found myself unable to articulate it at that moment.

Billy considered himself fortunate to have attended one of the top schools in his province.

"It was one of the few African schools equipped with a laboratory," he said. A mischievous smile played on his lips. "The only experiments we did were simple tests, using litmus paper to determine the acidity or alkalinity of different solutions. The first time I encountered beakers and Bunsen burners was in Mr. Paris's chemistry labs."

I found solace in the fact that Billy and I had finally initiated a meaningful conversation. Over the preceding four years I had lacked the courage to delve into substantial discussions. I was too afraid to subject myself to the scrutiny of others, too much a coward to confront the complexities that had plagued our relationships. What if it goes poorly? What if it only makes the situation worse? Perhaps it was better to leave well enough alone. Now that Billy and I had started a conversation, I was encouraged to be more candid.

African students resented the idea of our university's merit-based selection criteria. Of the one hundred successful candidates admitted each year, approximately eighty were of Indian descent. I cannot recall the exact means by which I broached this subject, but after a moment of self-reflection, there was a visible expression of alarm on Billy's face.

"Well, it's quite evident, and it does leave me bitter and angry. We live in an era of winners and losers, where the odds are stacked in favor of those who are already privileged," he said.

"But Billy, if I truly desire something and work diligently towards achieving it, isn't it fair that my hard work be rewarded in a manner that is equal to my effort? What is wrong with that?"

"Hard work is not the issue. We are capable of working hard too, but we were not given the same opportunities as you. Our possibilities were limited. They say you can make it if you try, but inequality exposes the lie behind that promise."

The conversation grew more serious, and I was careful to avoid making any frivolous remarks. "Billy, I hear you, but I think about my ancestors who arrived in this country with nothing more than the clothes on their backs. They refused to accept their status as slaves. Instead, they worked hard to establish their own schools, and they placed great value on education."

"And here's what Verwoerd, the architect of apartheid, had to say about my ancestors: 'Why tantalize African people with the promise of a better education when they are merely meant to perform menial labor?'"

We drove past a small village and Billy gestured towards a collection of huts with rounded, whitewashed walls and thatched roofs.

"A child born in this village is five times more likely to die in its first year of life. The child's mom is more likely to die during childbirth as well."

"I understand, Billy."

"Look, there are no schools here, just poverty and disease."

"That is what we need to change," I said.

"It's a rigged game, Ganesan. Our education is like a marathon. Only those who cross the finish line first are considered winners. They win because they have won before, and they have won before because they were given a head start in the race. African students were left far behind at the starting line: we were never given a fair chance. It's nothing short of a miracle for even one of us to secure a spot in a place like medical school."

I listened in agitation, with a fraught sense of unease rising inside. This was the first time I had heard meritocracy challenged so eloquently, and I was grappling to find an appropriate response.

"This merit-based system is not of our making," I said. I hoped that by protesting an injured innocence, Billy would be reassured that Indian people were not as culpable as he might believe.

I turned my gaze away for a moment and looked out of the window. I contemplated how my privileged middle-class upbringing had paved the way for my pursuit of excellence. I attended well-resourced schools, was surrounded by teachers who nurtured my talents and creativity, and I had a family who prioritized education above all else. It was all too easy to fall into the narrative that if I worked hard enough, twice as hard enough, I could transcend the barriers and attain some semblance of respectability. I clung to the belief that in becoming a doctor I would free myself from the shackles of apartheid. I could no longer ignore the glorified culture of achievement that I so shamelessly embraced. I began to realize that meritocracy was a path strewn with uneven hurdles, and was toxic to those who were less privileged than myself. I longed for Billy to understand that I recognized the inherent unfairness of it all.

Despite all that, it was difficult for me to abandon something that I believed had spurred me on towards success. Understanding did not equate to acceptance. Was it meritocracy that was evil, or was it the uneven hurdles that were the culprit? It was complicated, however. I hoped for a more promising narrative of meritocracy, one that would invest in and uplift education, rather than impeding the efforts of diligent and hardworking people when change eventually came to our country.

It became darker, and thunder rolled in the distance. There was so much more that I needed to discover. Billy's perspective would help me understand the undercurrent of tension that existed between us, tension that led to the suspicion that some amongst us were not fully committed to the struggle. The contours of our conversation had had taken on the nature of the fog outside, and broaching such a topic was bound to touch a nerve. I was relieved that our journey had come to an end.

Upon our reaching Montebello Hospital, a ferocious thunderstorm had broken, trees thrashed violently outside, and torrents gurgled through the gutter downspouts. The electricity was down, and the place was blanketed in darkness.

We spent dinnertime in the glow of a flickering kerosene lamp that smoked the faces of the all-masculine company. The hospital's sole doctor, an eccentric figure, wore bell-bottomed jeans and had shoulder-length curls. He tantalized us with tales of his surgical prowess and his myriad responsibilities. In addition to performing surgical operations, he attended to emergencies, did all the admissions, delivered babies, and cared for the fragile newborns.

After dinner Billy and I settled on the floor, captivated by the doctor's peculiar manner. With a yoga-like posture, he lay flat on his stomach, elbows bent and chin resting in his cupped hands. A musty scent wafted out of the antique stained pages as he reviewed anatomical drawings in preparation for the following day's procedures.

"Who would put the patient to sleep?" I asked.

Without raising his gaze from the book, the doctor replied, "I will induce the patient to sleep, wash up, go over to the other side, and perform the operation."

"Who would oversee the anesthetic?" Billy asked.

"One of the nurses will," he said.

A lightning bolt flew from the rooftop, down a copper wire, and into the ground outside. Billy's face kept appearing and disappearing as we sat on through the evening and listened to the doctor's bragging.

In the early hours of the following morning, at around 5:30, I was jolted awake by frantic knocks on the door.

"Hey *Dokotela*, there is an emergency in the outpatient area. You must come right away and see," implored a voice that heralded misfortune.

I rushed to the scene. The doctor was already attending to a distraught mother and her child. The ferocious storm had left its mark on both humans and animals alike. Their hut had been reduced to ashes, forcing them to seek refuge beneath a towering stinkwood tree. The mother bore burn marks on her chest, and she had just been given the devastating news that her child was dead. A snake had fallen out of a tree and onto the child. The child had succumbed to a snakebite.

Later that morning, Billy and I joined a group of nurses for an outreach clinic. Our journey took us along treacherous roads riddled with deep ruts, with sections that were almost completely washed away by the heavy rains. The morning sun cast a dazzling glow on the tin roofs of nearby homes, while tendrils of smoke intertwined with the mist that rose gracefully from the surrounding hills.

We arrived at our destination, a vast open space on the top of a hill. Hundreds of patients had already lined up, and were waiting for us. The ambulance door was opened wide to create a makeshift barrier, a secluded area where we could conduct examinations. A table was opened out. Nurses diligently checked pulses, recorded blood pressures, and jotted down notes on flimsy pieces of cardboard. I put on my white lab coat and placed a stethoscope around my neck, pretending to be a real doctor. I auscultated chests, listened to the rhythm of beating hearts, illuminated eyes with our trusty lights, and palpated the bellies of expectant mothers. There were instances when a nurse would help me adjust a patient's blood-pressure medication because they were more familiar with that than I was.

It was a few days later, during another stormy night, that the opportunity arose for a more private conversation with Billy. It was rather naïve of me, but I believed that he had been suitably primed, and I approached him with confidence and purpose.

"Billy, I wonder if you believe that Indian students are as equally committed to boycotts as African students?"

He stopped as though he had been struck by lightning, turned menacingly toward me, and answered with an irritability that threatened an explosion.

"This is Africa. Nobody truly cares about the plight of African people. Look at my community. See how we live, in huts that are at the mercy of the elements, with one doctor for thousands of people. Once you're done here, you will acquire your Mercedes Benz, purchase a grand house, and return to serve the interests of your Indian community."

I was frightfully offended, crushed by the intensity of his emotions, regretting that I had stirred such wrath in him, and wondering how I could extricate myself from this tangle. In that moment, though I was born in South Africa, I felt the weight of being a guest in an unfamiliar land, a temporary sojourner, and someone who was less from Africa than Billy was.

On the Richter scale of commitment to protests and boycotts, my needle usually oscillated between a tremor and an aftershock, whilst that of African students tracked a more seismic intensity. If you had seen us during a protest march, you would witness a resolute and defiant group who were united in their opposition to apartheid. However, what remained concealed was the inner turmoil and conflicting emotions that plagued me—the struggle of a middle-class boy who was too affluent to benefit from charity, yet not rich enough to enjoy the privileges of the wealthy. Each time I took part in a protest or boycott I risked missing exams, failing courses, forfeiting my scholarship, and with the potential for even being expelled from the university.

"Perhaps I'm simply impatient or intolerant, but I struggle to accept the lack of commitment by some individuals," said Billy.

"Our support for the struggle is without question. There's so much at stake," I said.

"Without struggle, progress is impossible. Those who desire freedom and discredit agitation are people who wish for rain but reject thunder and lightning. People in power will relinquish nothing without demands. Boycotting classes serves as a powerful tool to advance the struggle."

I felt myself more and more sick and dreary, too anguished to utter a word. I looked out into the troubled darkness.

Billy sighed. There was still fever in those eyes, but his voice took on a more apologetic tone.

"I understand how apartheid has fractured our relations and led us along divergent paths. Now is the time for us to come together as one. We must draw inspiration from our courageous colleagues like Steve Biko, people who paid with their lives."

Steve Biko, a charismatic former student of our medical school, tragically passed away after beatings while in police custody. The official cause of death: starvation from hunger-strike. His lifeless body, still restrained and stripped of clothing, was discovered in the back of a police vehicle, after he had been cleared to be transported to a hospital that was 740 miles away.

Biko advocated for a fresh perspective on our collective struggles as a people, a view that was untainted by the oppressive ideas perpetuated by apartheid. As the leader of the Black Consciousness Movement, he emphasized the importance of African, Coloured, and Indian people uniting under the banner of being Black.

"Whiteness is not the standard against which we should measure ourselves," Biko said. "We must embrace our Blackness as something inherently valuable, inherently beautiful, and a source of immense pride."

Then, in an extraordinary turn of events, Billy defied my expectations and ignited a discourse that proved as thought-provoking as any I had initiated.

"Liberation before Education, that strikes at the heart of the issue," he said.

I had encountered that slogan countless times in the past, but had often dismissed it. The very idea of questioning the value of education created a sense of unease, as my grandparents had instilled in me a deep reverence for learning. The mere thought of disrespecting education would have prompted them to demand I perform ten squats while crossing my arms and holding onto my earlobes.

Yet, hearing Billy articulate those words with such passion, I was forced to reconsider my stance. An idea that had been simmering in my head, and had been refined over time, suddenly droned its way into my consciousness.

"Liberation and Education are two sides of the same coin, intertwined and inseparable," I said. "If liberation is to hold any true meaning, it must bring about a transformative shift, and what better catalyst for such a transformation than education itself?"

"We cannot be misled by false pretenses and magical theories," said Billy.

"It's not a matter of magic, Billy. Change cannot occur in a vacuum. It needs to be supported by skills and capabilities that would sustain a new order."

"Hold on: I am not suggesting that education is irrelevant, just that liberation must take precedence. Remember, the overall goal is to dismantle apartheid. The necessary skills to bring about such change can't be acquired through books or lofty theories. We must engage with the struggle in a more practical way, one that would make us agents of historical change."

I couldn't escape the nagging thought that I had entwined myself in an evasive argument, a convenient ploy that allowed me to arrange my world creatively, so that I could succeed within the constraints of the apartheid system.

Lightning crept under the door and forked in through every window. I lay in bed that night, beyond the reach of warm milk, and reflected on how difficult it was for African and Indian students to conquer the racial divide. I knew I must find a way of becoming an agent of change, but this would be difficult—perhaps impossible—because I could not surrender my convictions about education. It troubled me no end that I lacked a tribal identity in Africa: I was not Zulu, Xhosa, Batlôkwa… Despite claiming Blackness as my own, in the eyes of my African colleagues, I was still an *insider-outsider*.

These feelings set me apart from the masses and made me feel rejected, like I did not fully belong. Perhaps it was my own wounded vanity, my discontent, that made me inwardly acknowledge this feeling of rejection. There was no way to walk away or avoid it. It was part of my pain, part of my internal struggle.

CHAPTER 13

The Maharajah and the Sepoys

It was a bright spring morning with a clear blue sky—an ordinary day in the latter half of 1984, possibly August or September. I arrived at the front entrance of medical school at 7:45, expecting lectures to begin as usual at 8 a.m.

An acrid smell permeated the air as the remnants of the national flag lay smoldering at the base of the flagstaff. Seething students, gathered in small groups, were telling tales of horror from what had taken place at the medical school residence in Wentworth the night before.

Portia was clearly agitated, her fists clenched, her index finger raised at times as she told us what had happened to her.

"I lay in bed, reviewing in my mind the complications of infective endocarditis. Suddenly, there was a loud bang. It felt as if there were explosions, flares lighting up the night outside, or perhaps it was a firecracker. It was not as deafening as the time the Mobil oil refinery next door was bombed, but it sounded really serious," Portia said.

She was too afraid to investigate the source of the commotion outside her door.

"I convinced myself that it wasn't real. My hands were trembling. I curled up and pulled the sheets over my head."

She lay there, paralyzed by the fear that had gripped her.

"I heard footsteps in the corridor, doors slamming, then there were heavier footsteps and brusque voices. '*Ons sal skop die deur in op een.* (We'll kick the door in on one).'"

The sound of a door being kicked off its hinges was followed by a woman's rising protest that quickly choked into a shriek of anguish. Portia scrambled out of bed, mute at first, but steadying herself to gain some sort of control over the situation.

A wry smile crossed her face as she mulled over the amusing thought, "The police were so dim-witted that they could only count to one," she told us. Then her tone became decidedly hushed, "I tucked the remaining pamphlets into my panties."

Portia knew that such raids were typically carried out by male police officers. If the situation had demanded, she would have insisted on being searched by a female officer.

Portia became more confident, and approached the window with a sense of urgency.

"I drew back the curtains and tried quietly to remove the wrought-iron bars," she said. Portia's head shook in disbelief, panic etched across her face, "A police officer lurked in the darkness just beyond the barred window. Our eyes locked for a moment, and then he thrust his rifle against my chest. There was a deafening crash, my door was kicked open. They ransacked everything in their path, even emptied out my fridge and scattered the food across the floor," she said.

I listened intently but without any surprise. It was not unusual for the police to treat us in this manner. The students at the residence in Wentworth bore the brunt of the intimidation. They had to be ready to escape quickly, even in the middle of the night. It was part of the strategy to loosen the burglar bars, and prepare hideouts beneath manhole covers and within stormwater drains.

It was almost eight o' clock, and we proceeded to the L2 lecture hall, where an urgent meeting was scheduled. L2 was a classic lecture theatre that spanned two floors. Its incline was filled with impassioned students who occupied every available space in the aisles and the long rows of wooden desks. An unfurled banner displaying the words "Liberation before Education" partially obscured Professor Kane's vibrant chalk drawings from the previous day's anatomy lesson. I squeezed my way into the lecture hall and wedged myself into a narrow space in the last row.

The delegation that had been meeting with the Dean entered, and a hush fell over the room. The Dean was furious. She told them, "The act of burning the national flag on campus is a highly provocative political gesture. It's irresponsible and unbecoming of aspiring medical professionals."

A ripple of agitation spread through the student body: "Damn her," "Can't trust those who sit in Ivory Towers."

No day was appropriate for desecrating a national symbol, yet every day seemed suitable for burning the orange, white, and blue. Our lives were immersed in a political landscape. Every aspect of our lives, where we lived, where we studied, our leisure activities, our social circles, were all determined by politics. There was no escape from this reality. We carried a burden of responsibility that was far beyond our years. Burning the national flag was not a trivial choice. It was deliberate, and *intended* to be politically provocative.

The Students Representative Council President took to the podium. He was a good-natured and self-confident fellow, daring but principled, whose easy-going charisma made him a natural candidate to lead us. Silence reigned in the room. He leant forward and hunched his shoulders with a slouching dignity. Then he began in his usual drawling manner, as though he were spelling out each syllable in lisped monotone.

"Comrades," he started, but then stopped mid-flight and reloaded, as though his tone lacked the trajectory required to propel the more lethargic amongst us.

"Comrades…Comrades, an injury to one is an injury to all."

His voice deepened and the words spiraled across the room like projectiles, capturing as they went the complete attention of the audience. "Comrades, they attacked us without provocation, whipped us as though we were animals, overturned bookshelves, toppled tables, scattered our textbooks, and ripped up our lecture notes. What did we do to deserve this?"

Some students stomped their feet and others pounded their fists on the desks. The quivering anger which had broken out in the aisles now swirled throughout the room.

The SRC president waved his hand to impose silence.

"Comrades…Comrades, we must become *conscientized*, understand that to be agents of change takes sacrifice."

I remember the very first time I heard the word "Comrade." It startled me. I have heard the word hundreds of times since, and it alarms me just the same. I find in its resonance a distinct military undertone that evokes a blend of attentiveness and apprehension. It also startles me because the apartheid regime had crafted a narrative that intertwined comradeship with communism, and communism with terrorism. I reject the notion of being labeled a terrorist or a communist. I am neither of those things. Yet I cannot deny being a comrade, in the true sense of the word.

The leaders in the fight against apartheid anchored themselves to the steadfast principles of logical rigor, drawing inspiration from the selfless acts of heroes such as Tambo, Biko, and Mandela. They reminded us of our enduring history of subjugation, emphasizing the relentless struggle for equality, and our unwavering resistance against conquest.

More than anything, student leaders were skilled at dispensing prescriptions of easily-digestible phrases that underscored the urgency of the situation. Awareness in itself was not enough. It required the use of powerful words, such as 'conscientize,' to enunciate the truth in a more meaningful way. Like freedom, fairness, and justice, 'conscientize' was more than just a word. It offered a perspective, and those among us who suffered from malaise and inaction needed to be given the right perspective.

Now that we were sufficiently primed, conscientized, we poured out of the lecture hall and spilled onto Umbilo Road. Spurred on by the powerful strains of *Tshotsholoza*, we marched down the road that was cleared of traffic on both sides. There was no force that ignited the fire of activism more than that Ndebele freedom song, which held a dual message: to move forward, and to make way for others.

Leading the procession were fearless individuals, stomping their feet and dancing the *toyi-toyi*, chanting defiantly behind banners that proclaimed 'Say no to Racism,' 'Defy Apartheid,' and 'We Will Overcome.' I was somewhere in the middle of the procession, surrounded by mostly Indian students, yearning for the seemingly impossible: to be embraced as a comrade while wrestling with the pervasive fear of being permanently excluded from medical school. At the back were those who exhibited the hesitancy of reluctant followers, their feet dragging with uncertainty, some driven out of lecture halls by the threats of having their names publicly posted, or being labeled as traitors to the cause.

We marched onward, fueled by the commanding voices that resonated from the front of the procession.

"*Amandla* (power)," they cried out.

"*Awethu* (is ours)," we responded in unison as we collectively thrust clenched fists into the air.

Our procession came to an abrupt halt at the intersection of Umbilo Road and Francois Road. An arc of terror lay before us. At its core was a line of the dreaded military Casspirs, with helmeted policemen peering out of hatches, their rifles trained on us. Alongside them stood Black policemen armed with *sjamboks* (whips), with muzzled Alsatians straining at their leashes, their menacing growls demanding that they be set free on us. There were White policemen in bullet-proof vests, crouching alongside teargas launchers that stood loaded and at the ready.

A burly commandant, with an unruly moustache and eyes concealed by dark glasses, raised the loudhailer, his voice crackling through, with a thick accent, "This is an illegal gathering. You must disperse immediately."

I felt afraid that the police would open fire at any moment, and with live ammunition. Yet, in the company of defiance, I was not deterred by the commandant.

We responded with resounding chants of "Viva Mandela Viva, Viva Mandela Viva!"

The commandant sounded exasperated, repeating his warning with even greater authority. We stood our ground repeating the rallying cry, "Viva Mandela Viva, Viva Mandela Viva!"

There was nothing that provoked the police more than the mention of Mandela's name. Yet, under the shields of our white lab coats, we persisted in unleashing a barrage of "Viva Mandela Viva!"

If on the previous night the police could only count to one, that morning their ability to count was lost altogether. There was a sudden *pop*, and a large, soft-drink-sized teargas canister arched above my head before descending into the crowd behind me.

At first, I struggled to make sense of what had just happened. I was caught off guard, startled and disorientated, unprepared for such a violent response. Then the adrenaline kicked in and I began to run back towards medical school. My eyes burned, my skin felt on fire, and the air in my lungs was squeezed out. I tried to cover my eyes with my lab coat, running blindly, in a panic-driven state. I scrambled around a second-year student who had taken a bullet to the thigh and veered clear of a police dog that was tearing into the leg of another. There was no time to stop and render assistance, just a primal fight-or-flight survival response. I ran this way and that, erratically trying to avoid the rubber bullets that whizzed by, and the flailing *sjamboks* that cracked the morning air.

In a desperate bid for safety, we ran towards the refuge of the medical school, fully aware that the police had always respected that boundary. Students streamed into upper-floor laboratories, lecture halls, common areas, and the cafeteria, seeking shelter wherever they could. I was too afraid now and wanted to get as far away from the police as possible. I slipped in through the back entrance of the hospital and went into Hut 4, where I pretended to interview patients.

That day, the police broke all protocol. They never entered the hospital, but pursued students into the university, beating them with *sjamboks* and allowing their dogs to run amok.

It must have been about an hour later when I hobbled back toward the campus in search of Adashnee. An eerie calm hung in the air, a disorienting aftermath that felt both unsettling and suspicious. Though the police had long retreated, the spoils of injustice, hatred, and discontent lay scattered around like the aftermath of a storm. Shards of shattered glass littered the place, and drying splotches of blood resembling spilled red wine covered parts of the concrete floor. A few shell-shocked students hung around loosely, scattered and immobilized, like spent cartridges, amongst overturned chairs. In the common area, only the faint rustle of the wind through the leaves, the withered Calla lilies in their now-dried beds, and the hushed murmurs of distressed voices remained.

Later, I spoke with Adashnee. She had run downstairs, alone, into the anatomy dissecting hall, and hidden among the dead bodies.

"Heavy boots thumped on the ceiling above, Alsatians panted at the door, and I could hear brusque voices in the hallway. The door creaked open for a moment that seemed like an eternity," she said. Perhaps it was the stupefying sight of the rows of dead bodies or their cadaveric smell that was enough to repulse both men and dogs.

It was hard not to perceive every situation as an opportunity for moral judgment, a stark distinction between those who shape history with a pen, and those who embody it with their blood. I couldn't escape the gut-gnawing guilt, the internal torment of feeling relatively unharmed, as if burdened by a sense of disloyalty, as if I had committed a crime by being unscathed. The absence of bruises, grazes, gashes, or scars only intensified my yearning for a visible sacrifice, something tangible to validate my commitment. As much as I had given, I still did not feel as though I had done enough.

That night I woke up—though I had indeed not been asleep, but lying half-conscious. My head was full of fumes, and the images of the previous day hovered above me like something that was in the far-away past. Then it all came back to my mind at once, as though everything had been lurking and ready to pounce upon me again, that night and for many a night thereafter.

In the days following the protest march, as we continued to boycott classes, I remained at home, seeking solace and contemplating my next steps. During those quiet evenings, when dinner was done, my parents would cast concerned glances in my direction, their eyes filled with an earnest plea.

"Krish, you mustn't involve yourself further," Ama said. Her voice was laced with worry. "This is not our way. Why would you willingly make yourself a target?"

"How can I possibly stay uninvolved, Ma? Not joining the African students would imply that we were siding with the White authorities. If we have any hope in this country, we will have to stand together with African people," I said.

Ama foresaw only the most dreadful and alarming consequences, and suffered accordingly. Recognizing her inability to sway me on her own, she turned to Dad, her lower lip trembling with indignation.

"This is going too far! Every night I've cried to sleep. It's all your fault. As the head of our family, you should have set a better example. You should have been a stronger role-model. Please talk some sense into him. Help him understand that his education is the only thing that matters."

Dad remained silent, like a human piñata, absorbing it all as Ama recklessly unpacked her frustrations. He was a timid man, yielding—but only to a certain extent. He could accept a great deal, even of what was contrary to his convictions, but there was a certain point beyond which nothing would convince Dad to deviate course.

Despite everything, Dad did not respond to Ama's outburst. Then, like a man regaining consciousness, he addressed me with a curious expression of sincerity.

"Consider this, Krish. Many young men convince themselves that they, and only they, have extraordinary beliefs. Beliefs are admirable, and strong beliefs even more so. But let me tell you with the confidence of a rather stupid man, a poor role-model if you may, that there is a point at which those beliefs can tip over into fanaticism. You are just a pawn in this dangerous game. It is easy for someone as young as you to be swept away by fanciful ideas. Think about what will happen when you overstep your bounds. Consider what you stand to lose," said Dad.

With frustration coursing through my veins, I sank into the sofa, my elbows resting on my knees and my face buried in my hands. It was challenging to heed the cautionary words of my parents. They belonged to a generation that had grown accustomed to submitting to White supremacy, and were content with being compliant citizens in a fractured society. Our world was undergoing profound changes, but their perspectives were out of touch with the harsh realities of the ongoing struggle.

They did not understand that activism was a deliberate and calculated process, something that was far from the recklessness that it was mistaken for. We understood that dismantling an unjust system required more than simply cutting off the head of an unjust King. We needed to engage with every facet of the system, resist it on multiple fronts, and stretch its resources to exhaustion. Only then could we envision the King as someone stripped of his defenses, vulnerable and isolated, and deposed from the status of a lofty deity to that of a fallible human being.

Despite my determination, I felt stung by certain truths in their arguments. I had to admit that, though it was against my nature, I had become increasingly impulsive and impatient, and at times I rebelled for no good reason.

My pride was wounded, and I felt seized by shame. All night I tried to nurse the resentment and self-torment that swirled in my head. I understood with certainty the implications of my actions. Skipping lectures, with exams looming one after another, filled me with concern. It could be weeks, even months, before we returned to the classroom, and I was fearful that my scholarship from MSD (Merck Sharp & Dohme) might be revoked. How would I finance the remainder of my studies? My father was unemployed, and we had no home to secure a mortgage against. Who would lend me the money? Each worry led to more worries—infinite spirals of fear.

One week after our protest march, shortly after lunchtime on another bright spring day, we gathered outside the British Consulate in Smith Street, Durban. Within its walls, four influential leaders of the United Democratic Front coalition were taking refuge.

A confident and defiant crowd several thousand strong stood beneath the imposing presence of Shell House that cast a long shadow over the scene. What had once been a disparate coalition had now merged into a formidable force, marked by an unexpected diversity. There were men in purple robes, their fingers devoutly keeping count with rosary beads, alongside portly matrons in burgundy jerseys, eagerly stretching on their tiptoes for a better view. Smartly dressed legal professionals peered upward through thick glasses, while street cleaners in drab overalls clutched their brooms. Amidst them all, a barefoot vendor balanced a basket of vegetables on her head, and a throng of university students in jeans and T-shirts raised their fists and voiced their protest with passionate shouts.

One of the men who had sought refuge inside the consulate was Mr. Ramgobind, the man who had introduced me to that strange and asymmetric variant of chess—'The Maharajah and the Sepoys'—where the powerful white king stands alone, opposite a full complement of black pieces in their conventional positions.

The police stood stripped of all motivation, weary and drained, their faces dressed in a strange humility. I attributed their inertia to the presence of international television crews broadcasting the scene. But there was something deeper at play. The limits of the 'White King' were now being defined by the solidarity and endurance of the 'Sepoys' he oppressed. The significance of the Maharajah and the Sepoys was now clear, and checkmate could not be far off.

CHAPTER 14

An Ethical Dilemma

In the period after the Consulate showdown, growing resistance was met with growing repression. The 'White King' might have been backed into a corner, but he refused to concede. In 1984, in response to an increasingly unified coalition of Africans, Indians, and 'Coloured' people, the apartheid government enacted legislation to establish the Tricameral Parliament. The move employed the age-old strategy of 'divide and rule', by dangling the promise of limited self-governance for Indian and Coloured people. However, the segregation laws remained unchanged, and the plan deliberately excluded the twenty-two-million-strong African majority.

It was a divisive period in our communities. A handful of Indian and Coloured people stepped forward as candidates for the new dispensation. They argued that they would work from within to bring about the necessary changes that would eventually include African people. Most people regarded these candidates with skepticism, believing their actions to be motivated by self-interest.

In the weeks leading up to elections for the Indian and Coloured Chambers of Parliament, I found myself back on the streets. Armed with a stack of pamphlets, I strode down John Dory Drive in Newlands East, a Coloured township and a so-called 'modest' neighborhood with recently-built semi-detached homes. As an Indian person I felt apprehensive about walking through this unfamiliar part of Durban.

I took a deep breath as I approached the first house, steadied myself, and rang the doorbell. No one answered, even though I could hear the television. I knew they were home, so I rang the doorbell twice and then two more times. After ringing yet again, I slipped a pamphlet through the space under the door.

I took a short cut across a small grassy divide that led me directly to the house next door. I rang the doorbell and could hear the chiming in the hallway. I rang again and still no one answered. Perhaps I'm not going to be speaking with anyone today, I thought, as I turned back towards the road.

The door cracked open, and a man and a woman appeared in the doorway. I walked back up towards the door.

"What's this in regard to?" asked the lady at the door. She sounded agitated. How could I blame her? This was a time when people were suspicious of others. What was an Indian guy doing in a Coloured neighborhood?

"I was hoping to get a moment of your time, ma'am," I said. I tried to sound casual as I readied the script that was in my head.

"We don't have time for this," the man said. He was dressed in a vest and shorts and looked like he had worked the night-shift.

"I'm a medical student, and I'm hoping that people will not vote in the upcoming elections," I said.

"You Brazzous (slang for 'young men') don't have anything better to do," he shouted, and slammed the door shut.

I heard the snarl of a dog inside and hastened my pace. I was almost at the road when an Alsatian came charging after me.

Despite the man's reaction, I was convinced that our message held weight. Equal participation within a unified and inclusive system was an idea worth sharing, even at the risk of being attacked by dogs. Each pamphlet that I distributed, and every conversation that I had, held the potential of planting the seeds of change.

Fewer than one in five Indians voted in the Tricameral elections, yet this did not prevent Indian people from facing the disdain of many African people. They labeled us all as 'sell-outs.' While I had aligned myself with the African majority, and fully embraced my identity as a Black person in South Africa, I could not escape the complexities of being an Indian person. Once again, I found myself stuck in the middle, sandwiched between White and Black communities.

The year following the Tricameral elections was a turbulent period. There was unrest in many parts of the country. The newspapers reported the clashes in African areas in the old colonial ways: as 'tribal conflicts' and 'faction fights,' and described them as "part of their lifestyle." There were rumors about a covert 'third force,' the hidden hand of an apartheid government that was orchestrating violence within the townships.

In early August of 1985 the murder of a prominent Black human rights lawyer in Umlazi, a township near Durban, ignited a wave of fear that swept through our region. Disturbing accounts emerged of African mobs advancing towards Indian areas in Inanda and the Phoenix Settlement. There were reports of home invasions and businesses being set ablaze. These were uncertain times, and progressive voices tried to reassure Indian people that the violence was not directed specifically at them. However, a sense of unease lingered within me. I knew that those of us who occupied the middle ground would eventually find ourselves caught in the crossfire. My thoughts drifted back to 1949, and I grappled with the same fear that haunted my grandparents' generation.

A few weeks later, on a chilly August evening, the men of our neighborhood gathered in the park at Bhoola Road, in Effingham

Heights. Among them stood an Indian police captain, a familiar face from our community. The atmosphere crackled with tension.

"Listen up," the police captain said. His voice was measured, his tone urgent, underscoring the seriousness of the situation. He adjusted his cap, tapped his baton against his palm, and surveyed the assembled crowd. "The escalating violence in the townships is deeply concerning. The situation is tense. We need to be vigilant. Our safety and the safety of our community hang upon it."

The Captain continued, his voice gaining in strength: "We must stand together. The law is clear. You have the right to defend your loved ones, your homes, and your livelihoods."

The fear of the police that I had acquired as a child had morphed into distrust and animosity in my youth. The government often deployed them as a tool to suppress even the slightest dissent. I came to listen to what the police captain had to offer because I wanted to know how I could shield my community from the genuine danger posed by angry African mobs.

The laws of our land mandated that every able-bodied White male undergo military training, whilst people of color, including Indians, were excluded. White families enjoyed a relative sense of security. In the event of an uprising by the majority, they were armed and prepared to defend themselves. I had never set foot in a military training facility, nor had I ever held a rifle. The prospect of facing an assailant was daunting. What would I do if I were to be confronted by such danger? How would I defend myself and those I cared about?

Many African people regarded Indian people as cowards, weak individuals who would flee at the first sign of trouble. This stereotype, coupled with our lack of meaningful defense, rendered us particularly vulnerable. I felt disheartened that these African people viewed my community and me as easy targets, people who lacked the courage and means to stand up for themselves. The weight of our vulnerability, and the limitations imposed upon us, were ever-present reminders of the challenges we faced. It was a constant struggle to navigate a society where strength was defined by the color of one's skin and the weapons at one's disposal.

The repugnance of what needed to be done, even when presented with the virtuous intent of self-preservation, was dreadful. I lacked any clear direction, but the idea of a self-styled armed guard filled me with uncertainty.

As the night progressed and fear eclipsed rational thinking, small clusters of neighbors took up positions along the perimeter of Effingham Heights. Our group was assigned the midnight to 4 a.m. shift. We prepared ourselves for the long night that lay ahead, uncertain of what we might face, and the toll it would take on us.

One of the neighbors brought Nunchaku sticks, another wielded an axe, and I grabbed the driver from my Wilson set of golf clubs. So, there we were in the dark of night, standing sentinel along the boundary line of Effingham Heights. At times an orange flicker of burning cigarette ends marked our huddle, and at other times one would notice the silhouettes of men fighting off the cold by adopting karate poses, felling imaginary trees, or playfully teeing off fallen acorns into the silent night sky.

There was a moment when I thought I heard the faint sound of drumming. Then there was silence for a minute or two, before it was there again, clearer, louder, closer. Dark, agonizing ideas rose in my mind. Was it part of an ancestral war dance, a tribal ritual before an attack? A dreamy fear began to gain mastery over me. I was reminded again of the scenes that had played out in 1949. The night was dead and silent, and I grasped that there were no drums, that the sounds I had heard were just my imagination.

The mornings were particularly difficult. I struggled to pull myself together. This new regime of midnight vigils, sleepless nights, and predawn starts to long hospital shifts was wearing me down. Early one morning, I was on to my second cup of strong coffee when the telephone rang. The distraught voice on the other end was that of an old acquaintance from primary school.

I was disturbed to hear that three of his relatives had been murdered, "hacked to death by rampaging African men in Inanda." Another family member had suffered injuries and was rushed to King Edward VIII Hospital for treatment.

It was true then, those reports of marching mobs, home invasions, and burnings. All of them were true. Even worse: now there were murders too. I put my head in my hands, with exhaustion spreading through my limbs, and a sickly feeling filling me with horror. I imagined the calm pastures in the Inanda of my childhood, the serenity that was interrupted only by the occasional bellowing of a bull in the distance. It was impossible to fathom how tainted it had become.

In the Casualty department that morning, all reason had lost its currency. Each minute brought a fresh hell, delivered by never-ending streams of flashing red lights and wailing sirens. Orderlies and nursing assistants frantically ferried the wounded: a stab wound to the neck, a gunshot to the abdomen, the crown of a patient's skull cracked open with a machete, large lacerations to the legs, a stabbed chest, a stabbed abdomen…

Two Black policemen summoned me into the ambulance bay. They threw open the back doors of the police van, and I was overwhelmed by the putrid smell of a decomposing and maggot-laden corpse. The person (I could not tell if it was a man or a woman) had allegedly been stoned to death—a victim of vigilante justice, a perverse response to 'traitors' who colluded with the state. The body displayed a grotesque array of swellings: the head doubled in size, bulging eyes that stretched through bruised and swollen eyelids, a ballooning belly, and limbs that had the appearance of bloated tree trunks. I applied my signature to the form they put before me, to confirm that the person was indeed dead, as though the obvious needed to be certified.

I returned inside. There was an Indian man who had been brought in from Inanda. It was uncommon, though not against the law, for Indian patients to be seen at King Edward Hospital. While I never obtained confirmation, it seemed plausible that this man could have been the relative of my acquaintance.

I leaned over the injured Indian man. He opened his eyes and drew deep, slow, painful breaths. Blood oozed from a gaping laceration on his arm, and drops of perspiration trickled down his forehead. His eyes appeared lost in a distant fog.

"What happened, uncle?" I asked.

"For over a hundred years we lived in peace alongside African people, then without reason, they turned on us," he said. "The looting and the burning started suddenly…"

As I began infiltrating local anesthetic around the laceration and prepared to stich up the wound on his arm, he told me what had happened the night before.

His family had stayed up all night, watching the street in front, expecting at any moment that intruders would enter and violently evict them from their home.

"That's where we expected the attack to come from," he said, "from out front."

"My wife remained in the living-room with the children," he said. "She tried to keep them quiet. I lit a cigarette and walked up and down, from the sofa to the dining-room table and from the table to the kitchen, and back again," he said. For what seemed like hours, he paced, breathing heavily, panting, becoming soaked with sweat and dry again, giddy and delirious from all that turning.

"The minutes passed, and I could hear gunshots in the valley below. I darted over to the window from time to time and peeked out into the street. I saw more smoke and more flames from another house that was set on fire," he said.

"These were some of the most awful moments of my life," he said. "I never felt so terrified. I kept looking at my wife and my children, and wondered how we would escape this horrible situation. We couldn't wait for morning to come."

"It must have been two or three o'clock in the morning when the telephone rang. I could hear the panic in my brother's voice, then the line went dead."

"Out of nowhere, something came smashing in through the back window, a petrol bomb I think," he said. He described how the fire spread quickly through the wood-framed dwelling, bursting through the kitchen door, blistering the paint on the walls, and blanketing the room in thick black smoke.

They were oblivious to the danger that lurked outside, but "had to get out, quickly," he said. "I tried to gather a few trinkets, sentimental things, and in that panic, I fell and cut my arm."

He lifted his free hand, tracing a path up his crumpled shirt, over the only remaining button that preserved his dignity. He fumbled within his pocket, retrieving a faded black-and-white photograph. He held onto the soot-smudged image of his parents, and the sound of his labored breathing, the heaving in the chest that adrenaline produces, was now clear.

"It's all that I could save," he said.

"We got into the car and sped off into the burning night. I kept to the gravel side-roads," he said. They drove past smoldering homes in an emptied-out neighborhood, through the black smoke that cloaked the valley, and around the wreckage of burnt-out cars that littered the road. The Phoenix Settlement, the place that Gandhi built, my primary school, the printing press, and even Gandhi's original home, were all on fire.

My pager went off. I was needed in the operating room, to assist with yet another gunshot to the abdomen. Now that his arm was sutured, I briefly took his hand in mine and wished him well. A nurse took over and proceeded to apply the final dressings and administer a tetanus shot.

For the next hour I pulled on metal retractors as the surgeon delved deep into a patient's abdomen, removing bullets, sticking sutures into a lacerated liver, and examining lengths of bowel that he raised between his bloodied hands.

Later, I returned to the Casualty department to attend to an African patient who lay on a stretcher. There was an unpleasant odor of alcohol about him, his shirt was stained with blood, and his pant legs ripped. A gaping gunshot wound trailed a stream of blood down his calf. The bullet had entered through one side of his calf and exited through the other.

He scarcely took notice of my approach.

"*Kwenzenjani, baba?* (What happened, father?)" I asked.

He looked at me glumly.

"It will hurt a bit, *baba*," I said as I drew up some local anesthetic. His expression deepened into an indignant scowl.

"I don't care. You can't hurt me," he said.

I stopped, looked up in dismay, and set the vial of anesthetic down. I applied antiseptic to the wound. It must have stung, but he remained stoical. Through all my probing, packing, and poking, he remained completely indifferent.

"*Kwenzenjani?* (What happened?)" I asked again, in a tone that was neutral, the weight of his scornful reproach just a moment before lending a weariness to my voice.

He appeared almost cheerful now, as though he was liberated from the wickedness that had consumed him earlier. He raised his head, gazing furtively around the room to see if it was safe to speak.

"They forced me to do it," he said.

"Do what?" I asked.

"To attack the people who are occupying our Zulu lands."

"Who are they?" I asked. He did not answer.

It had been a difficult day at the construction site, he told me. Though it was only Tuesday, he felt tormented by a burning thirst, and it was that thirst which compelled him towards Mshayazafe, an illegal beer hall near Inanda. Just hearing that name Mshayazafe filled me with a profound sense of dread. Its meaning was clear: "Beat him to death." He sat up on an overturned paint drum and took refuge in a dark and dirty corner of the tavern. There were five or six other men, likely fellow laborers, who stomped their feet to the explosive rhythms of *Kwela* and *The Lion Sleeps Tonight*.

"Thandi, the lady who ran the place, was making *usu* (stewed tripe with dumplings)," he said. "She's a strong lady, that one, like man. I ordered some 'blue train'", a concoction made from fermented sorghum wheat, to which methylated spirits were added to speed up the brewing process.

Hearing the words 'blue train' brought a smile to my face. The real Blue Train was a world-class luxury train traveling between Pretoria and Cape Town. This was a trip that he could experience for a fraction of the cost.

"I chewed on *usu* and downed my first jugful of beer. Ah, that felt gooood," he said. There was another man in the room, he told me. He was sitting apart, sipping from his pot, and looking around the company. A collector of 'subscriptions,' he thought, a henchman of a powerful warlord, the kind that roamed freely in the area, extorting money from landlords and business owners, and handing over the funds to even more powerful tribal masters.

"I did not see the other men come in. They had guns and *pangas* (machetes). The 'collector of subscriptions' rose to his feet and approached the laborers, who were in various states of drunkenness.

"*Hlanza abezizwe*," he said. The men with the guns commanded that all foreigners (Indians, Mpondo, and Xhosa) be removed from the Zulu homeland.

"I had no choice. They would have killed me. I had to do it," he said.

"Stay out of trouble," I said as I applied the last dressing.

"No, tomorrow I must get my revenge on those who hurt me," he said. He never told me who had shot him.

The riots continued for a few more days, with the police noticeably absent, either unwilling or unable to intervene. Thousands of Indian people in Inanda and the Phoenix Settlement lost their homes.

Some found temporary lodging with family and friends, while others were accommodated in temporary shelters.

During the final days of the riots, unpleasant thoughts flashed through my mind, like lightning running across the night sky, too fast to process. I was especially troubled by my encounter with the African patient in the Casualty department. The images of that interaction needed to be slowed down, and each frame carefully examined, so that I could unravel what I was feeling.

A righteous person cannot make baseless accusations or indulge in slander. Yet even people of integrity are not perfect. As much as I tried, I could not shake off the haunting notion that this man must have been responsible for killing my friend's family. All that appeared so vivid and real in my mind. The way I felt did not alter the moral threshold of my duty as a physician, but I wished I had a fact, some little bit of evidence, something more tangible, that could pacify these thoughts that had wormed their way into my head.

I realized that the man's demeanor had forced me to see him as part of a larger collective, as one of 'them' who had turned against one of 'us.' Once again, I found myself burdened with the weight of being an insider outsider. I was a Black person who had aligned himself with the cause of all Black people, and now a certain group of Black people had turned on me, only because I was an Indian person.

CHAPTER 15

Agent of Change

My last two years of medical school were defined by persistent social unrest, and characterized by an unending succession of protests and class boycotts. Then, in early December of 1987, our final medical school results were unveiled. A single typewritten list was affixed to the noticeboard in the common area.

A sizeable crowd was gathered there, brimming with nervous excitement, jostling and straining their necks to catch a glimpse of their results. Towards the front, a group spotted their names, designated by "Dr.," and broke away into a charmed circle, twirling and gyrating with excitement. A few students, unable to contain their excitement, let out shouts of triumph, their expressions echoing with "OMG! OMG!" Amidst the flurry of emotions, some found themselves overwhelmed, their tears intermingling with laughter as they huddled together in lingering embraces.

I noticed Portia, fidgeting anxiously, swaying and rocking in anticipation.

"Can you believe that this day has finally arrived?" I asked.

"It wasn't an easy path, but worth every moment of self-denial," she said.

"Our era was exceptional, with the struggles we fought and the pressures we faced. Even until the very end, I feared that ongoing boycotts might prevent us from writing the final exams," I said.

"There was a moment when I too wondered if the protests and boycotts would force us to repeat a year. And now it's all over, and we're looking at our final results," Portia said.

"Will you miss being here?" My enquiry carried a hint of sarcasm.

There was a moment of perplexed silence. She looked at me with bemused curiosity.

"What kind of question is that? We've experienced so much here, created countless memories. Of course I'll miss it. But right now, I feel like I've earned the right to scream with joy."

As I moved forward, I felt a feverish sense of excitement rising within me. Even before I reached the front, I could see my name at the top of the alphabetically arranged list. I closed my eyes, took a deep breath, and allowed the reality of my achievement to sink in. In that moment, though it would not be outwardly evident, I too became engulfed by the same intoxicating euphoria that had taken hold of the others.

Oh, how I wished that the feeling could have lasted a bit longer, that I was able to express my joy without any inhibition. I felt like a chess player who had exhausted all their energy in navigating the tactical intricacies of the game, only to find a victory that was accompanied by a shallow satisfaction and a deflated sense of fulfillment.

Considering the utter intensity of my ambition, the gratification of being the first doctor in my family, and the realization of a lifelong dream, one would have expected the end of medical school to have been filled with overwhelming ecstasy.

"Will you miss it?" Perhaps that was a question directed more at myself than at Portia. I could hardly comprehend what had just happened, and 'missing it' was something I struggled to come to terms with. I felt empty now that medical school was finally over. My dream had come to fruition, and all that remained was to observe from a distance and admire it. What satisfaction lies in that? It was only the striving for more that kept my ego alive.

To be astonished by nothing is a mark of great intelligence, some claim. Perhaps it may serve equally well as a sign of great foolishness. During moments of intense joy—I cannot say why—a sense of melancholy invariably overtakes me. I've come to accept that each of us possesses a unique perception of the form and significance of our accomplishments, and there will always remain a residue of sentiment that eludes being expressed to others.

I hurried back home. Ama would be waiting, and burning with impatience.

Ama was beaming when she opened the door. There was no need to ask whether I had passed: it was expected, and she could safely assume the result. She put her hands together and raised them heavenwards. Then she hugged me tightly, with her voice ringing out like a bell to which triumph and joy had given renewed power.

"I am so proud of you. Finally, my son is a doctor," she said.

The bronze plaque with emboldened credentials—Dr. Ganesan. P. Abbu (MB ChB)—that Ama had imagined would be affixed to the entrance of our house, the honor of which she had been, for years, dreaming about, now danced proudly before her eyes. It pleased me immensely to see my mother so satisfied, that these paroxysms of pride and, as some may claim, vanity, were all justified. I trembled as I recalled the hopeless misery and anxiety that had weighed so heavily upon us: the wretched screeching of the old knitting machine, the countless days of watery mixed-vegetable curry, the broken-spirited haggling with Dad over money. All of those trials were now vindicated. Her life's ambition had come to fruition.

Though Dad did not express it as clearly as Ama did, I could tell, from his dewy eyes and the smile that had strayed onto his lips, that a feeling long unfamiliar to him had flooded into his heart. I embraced him warmly, heavenly images of Thatha's smiling face flashing through my head. My victory was a victory for all the generations that had struggled to get me to this point. It was a reminder that dreams don't die: they endure in one's children.

A crowd was gathering in our home: my siblings had just come back from university and school, next-door neighbors stopped by, and several aunts and uncles had arrived. An impromptu party was gathering pace. Samoosas and cakes were laid out on the table. Ama was busy frying *puri* and *patha*, delectable treats of fried bread made from wheat flour, salt, and water, alongside yam leaves plastered with a spicy chili-bite mix, tamarind, and lemon juice, before being rolled and sliced.

The telephone rang.

"It's for Dr. Abbu," my aunt said.

"Who is Dr. Abbu?" I thought.

While Ama had long envisioned that title for me, I had yet to fully grasp the significance of being addressed in such a manner.

The voice on the other end was that of Uncle Bala, my mother's sister's husband.

"Congratulations, Doctor," he said. "Who would say that you're a doctor now, Krish. Remember how naughty Poobal and you were, little rascals running about barefoot in the backyard in Duffs Road. And I'll never forget the time you both knocked nails into my mother's sitting-room furniture!"

"Don't remind me about that, Uncle Bala. We honestly thought that we were helping to fix the slats that had come loose."

It felt wholesome to be surrounded by family and friends, to reminisce about our past struggles while celebrating the present.

The following morning, I put on a pair of jeans and a dress shirt, smart, but nothing too fancy. As I drove to the medical school, I knew that there would be no formal graduation. In a final act of defiance, we chose to uphold the long-standing tradition of boycotting the graduation ceremony. The qualifying class from our medical school, the Black section of the University, was invited each year to the official graduation ceremony at the White campus, up the road in Howard College. Imagine how absurd it would have been to give honor to an institution that treated us so disrespectfully.

I was disappointed that I would never be presented with the certificate that would validate my qualification as a doctor. The university would withhold that in protest. However, I consoled myself that my registration with the SAMDC (South African Medical and Dental Council) would still allow me to practice.

I joined the rest of my 'graduating' class in the L2 lecture theatre. There were no robed dignitaries, no caps, no gowns, and no guests. Not even our parents were invited. Our names were not called, we did not pose for pictures afterwards, and there was no cheering. Instead, we were called, in alphabetical groups, to the front of the lecture hall, where each of us signed a printed copy of the Hippocratic Oath. That was it!

Later, after thanking our lecturers and professors, a few friends and I made plans to meet for a celebratory dinner at Mykonos.

Mykonos, on the Durban beachfront, was an all-you-can-eat Greek restaurant. It had only recently opened its doors to people of color. Under the strain of growing social unrest, the government began to relax some of the segregation laws: beaches became accessible to all races; we were free to travel on all public transport; and restaurants admitted patrons from all racial groups.

A young White lady escorted us to our table. She fiddled nervously with her pencil, keeping it in perpetual motion as though it were oscillating under the influence of a magnetic field. I detected a look of amazement in her face, even a hint of fear, as she took our drink orders.

"Would you like something to drink?" she asked.

"I'll have a passionfruit and lemonade," I said.

"Look at this guy. It's a celebration and he wants lemonade. Come on, have a beer—or wine at least," my friend Kandas said.

The others ordered beers, but I stuck with the passionfruit and lemonade.

"Looks like we are the only 'Charous' here," Kandas said. He liked referring to us by using the slang word for Indians, derived from the Afrikaans words *char*, meaning 'brown' (or 'burnt') and *ou* for 'male'.

"Agents of change, *annan*, agents of change" Kandas said. He'd switched to addressing me with the Tamil word for 'brother.'

I hadn't noticed when we entered, but as I glanced around the packed restaurant, I realized that we were the only patrons of color. To be more precise, we were the only 'Charous' there. Though the restrictions had been eased, people of color did not flock to White restaurants. The memories of segregation were so strong, the experiences so recent, that most people of color, and especially African people, did not risk the humiliation of being harassed or turned away.

I felt uneasy as I walked up to the buffet with my friends. It was an uncomfortable feeling, the kind that arises when one feels that one is being watched. Indeed, I was being watched. Through the corner of my eye, I could see a few of the White diners looking up from their tables, scrutinizing me with great curiosity. I felt the weight of their examination, the silent manner in which they appeared to be evaluating me, judging me, checking whether I met their standards, whether I was worthy enough to be present in such a place.

My friends and I had not gone to Mykonos to fulfill any socially-appropriate etiquette. We were curious to explore a place that was once forbidden to us; but more importantly, we were frugal students interested in getting full value for each of our twenty-five rands (about $12.50 in 1987).

The buffet held an impressive selection of salads, entrees, and desserts. I placed a few skewers of coal-grilled chicken souvlaki onto my plate and smothered it in tzatziki sauce. A few slices of spit-roasted lamb were added, and a piece of lemon-garlic cod as well. I could not resist the rice-and-herb-stuffed grape leaves; those were delicious, I was told. Grilled octopus! Wow, I've never heard of that before. Wonder how that would taste? I spooned a few pieces and delicately placed it to one side so that the flavor would not be altered by anything else. Soft cheese, honey-drizzled baklava drenched in spiced syrup… Without acknowledging that I could come back to the buffet as many times as I wished, I piled them all onto my plate—now heaped full.

I made my way back to our table, took my seat, and paused for a moment to appreciate the spectacle that sat on my plate.

A strange, senseless smirk came over the face of the lady at the adjacent table. Spite rankled in her voice, "Oh, they're letting Coolies eat in here now," she said.

I was struck, not so much by her blunt, derisive hostility, but that she had said it loud enough, making sure that we would hear. I was filled with seething anger, a fire that threatened to reduce her to ashes. However, I smiled, a contemptuous smile that subdued the beast that was rising within. Her provocation was not going to spoil my celebration.

In the year of my internship, I earned the princely sum of nine hundred rands ($450) each month, and twice as much in the month of my birthday. That was a considerable amount in 1988—when my little brown Ford Escort with its manual gearshift cost six thousand rands ($3,000).

Every week, Adashnee and I went to a different restaurant in Durban. We uncovered all the culinary delights that we had missed out on during our childhood, like when Dad would drive us down the Golden Mile at Christmas time. The menus did not have to be imagined. We could taste them for ourselves: the kingklip and tiger prawns at the Elangeni; grilled salmon, Teppanyaki style at the Sukihama Japanese Restaurant; smoked line fish, calamari and oysters at The Smorgasboard Grill; and risotto and pizza at Punchinello's.

Entering previously segregated spaces did not automatically guarantee acceptance, but there was no doubt that we had arrived, and we too were living the dream. Slowly, ever so slowly, we became more comfortable with eating in desegregated establishments, and it was my sense that White people became accustomed to us as well.

After a few years in my clinical rotations at medical school, all I wanted was to be an obstetrician gynecologist. By the time I had qualified, the one thing I knew I did not want to be was an obstetrician gynecologist. I had dreams of specializing in internal medicine, so that I too could practice in a majestic realm and invent fancy aphorisms like "It licks the joints and bites the heart."

My family's financial situation remained tenuous. It had been seven years since my dad had lost his job. He had tried to find employment, and had short-term work, but there was nothing substantial. My three younger siblings were in university: there were fees to be paid, books to be purchased. My parents had invested much into my success, and I felt the pressure to go out and earn as quickly as possible.

Private general practice would be one of the ways to achieve my goals, and in the shortest time possible. The doctor who stitched up my dad, when he had sustained that cut on his scalp, encouraged me to buy his practice, on Bailey Road in Redhill. He was returning to the university to specialize in pediatrics.

"You can always go back and do internal medicine," he told me. He offered to sell me the premises as well. "It's a big building that comes with an adjoining space that could be used as a general store. Your parents could run that," he said.

That sounded like a good proposal, but the weight of Billy's words forced itself vividly upon me: "When you're done, you will get your Mercedes Benz, buy a big house, and go back to serve Indian people." I felt the same rush of the feeling that I had experienced then. Those were accusations that I wished to erase. I wanted to prove, more to myself than to Billy, that I was a man of conscience, and that I was sincere in my convictions.

I resolved to pursue two goals. First, I would acquire the practice on Bailey Road and assist my parents to establish a general store adjacent to it. Once I had established myself, I would actively seek out an opportunity to practice in an under-served community. That seemed feasible, considering that the practice on Bailey Road primarily served medical-aid patients who attended in the evenings. That would leave the mornings free.

Six months after establishing my practice in Redhill, one of my patients, Mr. Dube, urged me to extend my services to Hillcrest, the nearest town to his rural community in Molweni.

The Clocktower Building in Hillcrest is about fifty kilometers northwest of Redhill. It stands in a prime location, at the intersection of two major roads: the access road to Molweni, that lay in the Valley of a Thousand Hills, and the Old Main Road that connects the cities of Pietermaritzburg and Durban. The moment I spotted it, I knew that it would be an excellent location for a medical office.

The hands of the Clocktower displayed 11:30 when I parked outside the building. It was a posh place, and I experienced the same nervous anticipation of someone who had stumbled upon their dream house. The place was occupied by a real-estate agency. Every fiber of my being hoped against hope that it would be available for rent, that no one would outbid me, that by some magical intervention it would be mine.

I got out of my car and looked around. On the opposite side of the road leading to the Valley of a Thousand Hills, I saw White people enter and leave Christiaan's, a grocery store. Outside the Standard Bank, on the other side of Old Main Road, stood a few elderly White men, and an African nanny pushing a stroller carrying a White child. Hillcrest was a White residential area, with White doctors who treated only White patients. How on earth would I be able to set up a practice in the heart of a White enclave, and one that would see mainly Black patients?

"You must be crazy," I said to myself. Yet this was a chance encounter, a neat coincidence, and held a fatal attraction for the impossible.

I entered the estate agency and told the receptionist that I was looking to rent the premises for a medical practice.

"Mr. Lindon wants to retire," she said. "He owns the agency and the building."

My hopes soared.

An elderly White gentleman showed me into his office, and I unfolded my proposal. He looked at me with surprise, and even disbelief that I would dare to consider such a possibility. I had barely sat down when he began getting up.

"I've got to think about that," he said, with a most businesslike, dry, and even contemptuously menacing tone. "You must really excuse me. I positively do not have another moment now. It's almost lunchtime, and another meeting beckons. Come back tomorrow."

I returned the following day. Mr. Lindon wore an expression of well-feigned irritability.

"I must admit I'm a tad uncertain: if you're quite familiar with what you're up to, and should you be inclined, the monthly rental would amount to five thousand rand ($2,500)," he said.

While medical school had equipped me with the knowledge and skills to handle heart attacks and diabetic comas, it had left me ill-prepared for the practical aspects of running a business. How does one negotiate a rental agreement? What's a line of credit? Should I lease or buy my car outright?

Perhaps Mr. Lindon felt that an offer as outrageous as five times the going rate would make me slink away and not bother him anymore. But this was a new age, and I was an agent of change, wasn't I? Though I might not be able to afford the rent, and would be rushing headlong into a path that might consign me to failure, I could not step aside, could not allow the landlord to hold the upper hand. No, I had to call his bluff and hold him to his honor.

Two weeks later I had signed the lease, and the Clocktower Building was transformed into a medical office.

"*Sawubona*," I said as I walked in on my first morning. There were about forty people in the waiting room: elderly men in dusty coats, crouched painfully over knobbed wooden staffs; older women, wrapped in traditional woven blankets, their faces smeared with ochre paste; a sleeping baby, tethered to his mother by a colorful flannel blanket, his snot-filled nose squashed against her back. There were a few women who squatted on the floor, and a young man who tried to ease the burning of gonorrhea by shifting impatiently from foot to foot. With so many people crowded together, the room felt very hot, and the air somewhat musty.

The nurses, whom I had interviewed the week before, were busy: Veronica was entering patient names and addresses onto large index cards, and jotting down brief entrance complaints, while Dudu readied the emaciated young man she had just escorted into the examination room.

The patient who sat on the examination couch was in his early thirties. He had already unbuttoned his shirt, and a hollow cough kept interrupting the flow of his story. His white handkerchief was stained with sputum that was mixed with blood. The fresh scars under his right breast signaled that he had recently sought the services of an *inyanga* (a traditional healer*)*. The etchings, made with the claw of a lion, summoned the forces beyond this mortal world, and remained an expressive record of the man's dark passage through his period of illness. I listened over these engraved signposts, and confirmed the telltale signs of pneumonia, a complication often associated with the HIV infection that was sweeping through South Africa. He required care that was beyond the meager resources at my disposal. I wrote a referral letter and sent him to the King Edward VIII Hospital, where I had trained.

The patients that I saw for a modest ten to fifteen rands ($5–$7.50) received in return a full assessment and all the necessary medication. At best, by month's end, I was only breaking even, but I would not have it any other way. The extent of their suffering was clear, yet the people of the Valley never complained, and were ever so grateful for the help they received.

More and more Black patients came, and their presence in the centre of Hillcrest was unmistakable. Their support of the White supermarket across the road ought to have been celebrated. Instead, the locals became unhinged, and complained: that the signage advertising my practice did not meet regulatory standards, and that my patients were loitering outside the Clocktower Building. I might not have fully complied with the bylaws, but there were no drunks stumbling about, no graffiti defacing public property, no shouting or aggressive behavior. People simply waited to catch the next taxi home.

About six months into my lease, the landlord approached me.

"You're a reasonable fellow," he said. "I don't want you to look upon me as a monster, as I have genuinely come to like you, old chap." He pondered a long while, time enough that I might absorb the generosity of his words. "I have complete confidence in your politeness as well as your discretion and good sense. Now, I come with a proposition, which I believe will be greatly to your advantage—and to my advantage too."

Though I had taken down the *Dokotela* sign that breached regulations, he still cited it as a violation of my lease. He proposed that I move to a smaller space at the back of the building, and though he did not suggest it directly, there was a veiled threat of legal action.

"That's simply ridiculous," I said, protesting the unfairness of his proposal. My head sank dejectedly. Agent of change perhaps, but how would I defend myself when the odds were stacked so heavily against me?

Within a month, I had been nudged out of the main building and into the obscurity of a smaller area at the back. Even when it rained, patients were forced to sit on benches outside. Over time, fewer and fewer patients came.

None of these changes appeased the landlord.

A few months later, as my first year's lease approached its renewal date, the landlord returned. He was more resolute now.

"I must inform you, in no uncertain terms, that I shall not be renewing the lease. It is expected that you shall vacate the premises entirely by that given time," he said.

I went from building to building in Hillcrest, searching for alternative premises, in what became a series of rejections. There was a glimmer of hope when the management of the supermarket building across the street considered renting out their storage space, but nothing came of that. Landlords simply scoffed at the idea of a non-White medical practice in the centre of Hillcrest. It felt as though there was a silent conspiracy, that property owners had contrived in some way to evict me completely.

Eventually, I did find a place, appropriately hidden from public view, on the second floor of an office block that was several hundred meters away from the Clocktower Building. The practice suffered even more, and what was fiscally a break-even proposition turned into a total loss. Still, I was determined to stay the course. In a way, all that had emboldened me, made me stand my ground and refuse to leave Hillcrest.

CHAPTER 16

The Dream Comes Together

It was a Friday afternoon in February of 1990, blazing hot and humid, and a dramatic thunderstorm was threatening Hillcrest. With only two months remaining until our special day, Adashnee and I were busy with wedding preparations. Just before I put the telephone down, she said, "I think I'll stick with red roses and white carnations for my hair. It will go well with the baby's breath."

"*Aibo! Aibo!*" I heard my nurse Dudu shriek. Could she really be exclaiming "unbelievable" in response to Adashnee's choice of flowers?

"*Aibo!*" she said once more. "Mandela's going to be freed from prison!"

The news of Mandela's impending release was not easy to embrace. There were several occasions when I had heard such rumors, and each time was left disappointed. Yet, observing the passion with which Dudu embraced the news, I began to believe that perhaps this time it was true.

The following Sunday afternoon, Dad and I were sitting in front of the television. The hours dragged on, and the camera lenses were focused intently on the gates of Victor Verster Prison. I found myself slipping into surreal moments of disbelief, finding it difficult to grasp the magnitude of what was unfolding before us.

The all-White television panel made repeated mention of "Mr. Mandela." I had become accustomed to the South African Broadcasting Corporation depicting Nelson Mandela as 'a menace to society' and 'a merciless terrorist.' Hearing the commentator utter the words "Mr. Mandela" attached a delicate, strangely elevated, and almost human connection to his name.

It was illegal to publish photographs of Nelson Mandela while he was holed up in his Alcatraz-like fortress on Robben Island. At medical school, we had so often chanted, "Viva Mandela," and held up placards bearing his name; yet if I had passed him in the street that day, I might not have recognized him. The person I imagined walking through those gates was the one pictured at the Rivonia Trial twenty-seven years earlier—a rugged, full-faced, scruffy young man who resembled a boxer.

The man who finally emerged, after insisting on his afternoon nap, appeared much older, taller, and leaner than I had imagined. Even in the fading evening light, his presence exuded grace and a dignified, grandfatherly elegance. I could only imagine the countless times the crowd must have exclaimed, "Aibo!" and the irresistible urge that propelled them to rush towards his motorcade, to touch the car carrying him, and to join the procession. Occasionally he would raise a triumphant clenched fist in the familiar Black Power salute. Throughout it all, he seemed unaffected, at least externally, by the blaring sirens, the flashing lights of the police cavalcade, and the swarm of reporters and television cameras that followed his every move.

Later, as I watched the news, I witnessed the vast crowd that had gathered at the Grand Parade in Cape Town. The words he spoke from the balcony that day resonated not only with those present, but with people across the globe.

"Comrades and fellow South Africans, I greet you all in the name of peace, democracy, and freedom. I stand here before you not as a prophet, but as a humble servant of you, the people…Amandla! (Power!)"

Mr. Mandela emerged as a beacon of moral leadership, a guiding light who would lead us through the challenging times that awaited. All my hopes and fears were projected onto Mr. Mandela.

This was unlike anything I had witnessed before, and it came at such short notice. It was truly an "Aibo!" moment, and one that filled me with awe, wonder, and disbelief.

It was April 8, 1990, a Sunday morning and our wedding day. At exactly 10:30, more than a thousand people gathered at the Merebank Tamil Society Hall, in Durban. The crowd was predominantly Indian—family, friends, neighbors, and even some of my patients.

The guests entered through a garlanded entranceway flanked on either side by freshly-cut banana trees. Women in elegantly draped silk saris, and adorned with 22-karat gold jewelry, held decorated wicker baskets, out of which they handed each guest a dainty little box filled with traditional pink-and-white sweets and sugar candy.

An attendant stepped forward and made some adjustments to the red roses and white carnations that were intricately braided into Adashnee's hair. Then, with the vibe of Carnatic music (South Indian classical music) filling the air, the guests stood up and turned their attention towards us. We walked down the aisle in procession: the *nadaswaram* (clarinet) players in front, Adashnee in a red Benares silk sari from Enen's, and I in my Pierre Cardin suit from Casanova. Our parents and grandparents followed closely behind.

We ascended the few steps onto the elevated stage, entering the grandeur of the *manavarai*, a magnificently-carved canopy supported by four pillars. The stage foreground was lined with glittering brass décor: marigold-garlanded pots that shared the space with giant *kuthuvilakkus* (oil lamps) crowned with peacock motifs, from whose fanned tails glowing wicks emitted a soothing light. On one side, a statue of

Lord Ganesha sat gracefully on a lotus throne, his trunk curved to the right, invoking the vibrant energy of the sun.

The priest sat cross-legged on the floor, chanting next to the *havan* (sacred fire). Adashnee and I took our places on a decorated bench, listening attentively to his pious advice, our hearts quivering to the incantation of Tamil mantras. Handfuls of rice and ghee were offered into the *havan*, setting off a joyous swirl within the sacred fire as the winds of heaven danced with our hearts. A tremor of intense excitement came over me as I folded my right arm around the back of Adashnee's shoulders and, in that sideways embrace, reached across and placed the dot of marriage on her forehead. Later, we walked around the ceremonial fire seven times, each round symbolizing a promise: nourishment, strength, prosperity, family, progeny, health, and loving friendship.

I had had an irresistible fancy, a mischievous idea, that when the time came to tie the *thali*—the sacred saffron string that symbolizes marriage and is tied loosely around the bride's neck—I would secure it with a surgical knot instead of the usual square form. When that moment arrived, I teased Adashnee with a naughty look and we gushed with laughter, a private little moment that remained a secret to the world. In the end, with the priest snooping with hawkish authority, I tied three knots in the ordinary way.

After exchanging garlands an auspicious three times, I took hold of the bamboo staff, a symbol of gallant courage, and guided Adashnee down towards the front of the stage. A queue had already formed of people eagerly awaiting their turn to offer congratulations, and to shower us with fragrant flower petals and colorful confetti.

Once we were done taking family pictures, we joined our guests for a traditional South Indian lunch. A convoy of servers went along the long rows of trestle tables, scooping out saucersful of vegetable biryani onto freshly-cut banana leaves, and placing ladlesful of dhal over the rice dish. There was salad—with grated carrots and radishes, spiced with diced green chilies, and infused with a healthy dose of vinegar. And what would such a meal be without the salty lime and mango pickles? Huge urns of water were boiling so that tea and *sooji* (a sweet dessert made from semolina) could be offered after lunch.

I saw in our union a promise that was ripe with possibilities—the security that comes with belonging so intimately, a sense of grounding, meaning, and continuity. Like snuggling up to the idea of a multiracial democracy, there was something complete, a satisfaction in renouncing our separate ways and embracing a life together as one.

Two years after Nelson Mandela's release from prison, in March of 1992, Adashnee and I were living in a basement apartment suite that was only two doors away from my practice in Redhill. It was an exciting time in our lives, as Adashnee was a few months into her pregnancy with our first child, Tharunamaya.

During this period, there was a flurry of 'behind the scenes' political activity. In an unexpected turn of events, the apartheid government called a referendum, to be held among the White electorate in South Africa. In a vote that stunned the world, the vast majority agreed that negotiations were to be started on dismantling apartheid. Plans were set in motion to facilitate free and democratic elections that would include *all* the people of South Africa.

In the weeks that followed, and while Adashnee struggled with morning sickness, there was much retching going on in the country as well. The mood was changing, and changing rapidly, as we appeared to be descending into a civil war.

In the Afrikaner heartland, burly White militants—some in khaki shorts and others dressed in battle-fatigues—brandished shotguns, clambered onto horses, and raised swastikas in defense of their covenant with God. Members of the AWB, a self-styled Afrikaner paramilitary group, resorted to acts of violence, planting bombs in Black taxi ranks and indiscriminately firing upon occupants of minibus taxis.

While the prospect of an ANC–led government held favor with most Black people, it was an apocalyptic threat to those who desired to revive the former glory of King Shaka and the Zulu nation. The long-standing animosity between the communities of Xhosa (largely associated with the ANC) and Zulu (aligned with Inkatha) resurfaced, leading to violent confrontations in the streets. Warlords roamed the suburbs and countryside, seeking to assert dominance by eliminating their rivals and imposing their authority on local communities.

Rumors circulated that a clandestine 'hidden hand' or 'third force' was also at play. Reports surfaced about the national defense force stockpiling weapons, and about covert operations: military-style attacks on trains, drive-by shootings, and political activists vanishing under mysterious circumstances.

The raised fists of the Pan African Congress punched the air with cries of "One settler, one bullet." This sent tremors through many White communities. There was panic-buying in the supermarkets in Hillcrest. Fearing the worst, people stocked up on canned foods, flashlight batteries, and other staples. The stores ran out of toilet paper. A Black patient shared that her boss had filled his swimming pool with drinkable water, just in case.

The months passed, and the violence escalated. We had lived through so much turmoil, and 'this too will pass.'

On September 2, 1992, I gazed into the innocent eyes of my precious bundle of joy. I was overcome with a profound sense of wonder that can only come with the arrival of one's firstborn. In the fragility and beauty of existence, I realized that the way I saw the world would be altered forever. Life could no longer be measured by adult aspirations. It would be a shared journey with a tiny, innocent being who depends on you for their every need.

In those silent midnight hours, while I was re-evaluating the world into which we had brought new life, the most morbid thoughts bounced about my head. I too began to feel the twitchiness that was spreading like a convulsion among Indian people. In place of that definite position that I so desired was fear, an uncertainty that once again called into question the issue of where I truly belonged.

Indian people had no claim to any tribal status in Africa, and no right to any ancestral land. Despite our support for the democratic movement, we were still considered outsiders. How cruel it all sounded now, this realization that the separation which apartheid had forced upon us had reinforced an Indian identity, and hindered our assimilation into a broader African identity. There was no crisis of being in terms of *who* I was. The crisis of being lay at the heart of *where* I felt I belonged.

I've often wondered how much a one-year-old understands the celebrations around their first birthday party. Is the party for the child or the guests? In defiance of that theory, Tharuna was walking confidently, and babbling away with kids and adults alike on that day in September of 1993. As Adashnee lifted a slice of birthday cake and transferred it onto a plate, the glow on her cheeks was noticeable, her complexion radiating a soft, luminous quality that comes with late pregnancy. Our second child, Kavithan, was due in November that year.

In that same month, September of 1993, we were also informed that a Transitional Executive Council was to oversee the country's move toward democracy. Elections were to be held early the following year.

On April 27, 1994, the day of the first democratic elections in South Africa, I was up early. Tharuna may have been free-spirited, but she suffered from the most terrible bouts of colic. There were times when the pain was so intense that Tharuna's lips would turn blue.

When the election coverage on the TV began at six o'clock, I was still rocking Tharuna, gently trying to induce a burp that would relieve the colic. Adashnee was lying awake in bed, with Kavithan cradled in her arms. The pictures on the television showed long queues of excited people—zigzagging across open fields in rural areas, and curling around urban street corners—buoyed by the opportunity of casting a vote for the very first time.

So much had happened in the preceding few years ,and now such radical change was coming into my life. All this set my mind racing with excitement, that thrill increasing now that Tharuna had finally burped.

After so many years of struggle, freedom—which for the longest time had remained beyond my imagination—was no longer something that I had just hoped for. It was here, it was real, and I could feel it. This was the moment when I would gain a rightful share of my country, the freedom to choose for better or for worse, a precious day in which I would, in a way, become the master of my own destiny.

Later that afternoon, Adashnee and I waited in line to vote at the library in Redhill. There were Indians, 'Coloureds', and African people, all standing together in a single line with a single purpose.

Some thought of this day as the day when apartheid finally died. As I waited in line, I looked upon it as a fresh start, and an opportunity that was filled with possibilities. I hoped for peace and prosperity in our country, and that I would be granted the courage to forgive the injustices of the past. I wished too that equal opportunity meant equal regard and respect for all. Above all, what I secretly desired was finally to feel that sense of belonging, my private place in the vastness of the universe that I could truly call home, and a realization that this was my country too.

After casting our votes, we took the kids to my parents' home in Effingham Heights. It was time for afternoon tea, a moment to unwind and indulge in one of our favorite tea-time treats: *bhajias*. Ama was busy chopping up onions and green chilies which were to be mixed with chickpea flour and water to form delectable little balls that would soon be deep-fried. Dad preferred coffee with his *bhajias*, and he liked it black. Ama favored tea, and it had to be white. "With extra milk," she would say.

Dad picked up a cigarette. "These will be the death of me," he said as he tapped on the end that was to be lit.

"You should give them up, Dad," I said.

"I don't drink, and what is there to take its place?"

"Wasn't it wonderful to vote," I said.

Dad nodded with some hesitancy, and a frown came over his face.

"You seem to be a bit bothered, Dad," I said.

He took a moment before responding, "I worry that we may be focusing on entirely the wrong thing. Freedom may appear to be glorious, but can it bring us happiness?"

Even Dad was struck by how frankly he enunciated those words. His support for democracy was without question, but he must have had serious misgivings, enough that he could come up with such a deep and weighty observation.

He took my hand and held it in his own, examining it as though he was searching for some familiar trait.

"At some point, you need to stop being a rebel. Climb down from that mountain of righteousness, and breathe the air of real life," he said.

"What do you mean, Dad?" I asked.

"Do you honestly believe that one man one vote is going to solve all our troubles at once?"

"We cannot know what fate awaits us, Dad," I said. "The best we can hope for is to have the freedom to make independent choices, whatever those choices may cost and wherever they may lead us."

"That may be true, but think about what will happen after Mandela is gone. Would we be forced to flee this country with only the clothes on our backs?"

"Dad, this is not Uganda. We must trust that things will be better."

The idea of freedom was seductive and clear. However, I had not considered the issue of happiness, nor whether it was indeed possible for a rebel to be happy. No, freedom did not appear to be synonymous with happiness. Dad was right: there was no guarantee that one person one vote would bring us the *happiness* we desired. Regardless, I had to believe that this would all work out. As a person who was stuck in the racial middle, what alternative did I have but to believe?

In an election that was remarkably free of violence, the African National Congress won by a landslide. Champagne flowed, fireworks filled the night sky, and crowds broke out into spontaneous dancing in the streets. The entire country breathed a collective sigh of relief.

Two weeks after the election, Nelson Mandela was inaugurated as the first president of a democratic South Africa. The Union Buildings in Pretoria, which are spectacularly framed by the lavender blossom of jacarandas in spring, provided a stunning backdrop for this historic event.

A flyover of jets painted a stream of colors to announce the birth of the Rainbow Nation. Mr. Mandela's personal praise-singer stirred the crowds with his mix of evocative verse and rhythmic songs. People chanted, "Madiba, Madiba," Mandela's Xhosa clan name, as the praise-singer extolled the virtues of the village herd-boy turned President.

Nkosi Sikelel' iAfrika (God Bless Africa) was adopted as our national anthem. The reverently acclaimed hymn had been an integral part of African liberation music, and now we too stood as one with other African countries that shared a common colonial experience. The anthem did much more than that: it sealed a great moment for reconciliation, a moment that connected people of all racial and political stripes. The air was filled with confidence. There was hope that a democracy achieved without violent revolution heralded peace and stability in our country.

Of all the dignitaries that were invited—presidents, princes, archbishops, and famous musicians—my attention was captivated by a shirtless, dark-skinned young man kneeling on stage with his hands symbolically bound in chains. Each time the camera panned across that poignant image, goosebumps rippled down my back. I was reminded of the psychological restraints that had kept us prisoners in such an abnormal social system. When those shackles were finally removed, their release was palpable. The wrongs we had received, first from three hundred years of colonialism, and then from apartheid, had finally ended.

Free at last, free at last: we were free at last!

Everything seemed so worthwhile now. Never had I felt so firmly anchored to this land: and for the first time I felt truly proud to be South African.

CHAPTER 17

Things Fall Apart

At around four o'clock in the morning, on a day in January of 1995, Mr. Singh called.

"Come quickly," he said.

I heard the distressing sound of his wife groaning in the background.

It was convenient to live in a basement apartment just two doors away from my practice in Redhill, but that did not spare me from the dangers of making house-calls in the middle of the night.

I went through the tedious routine: disabling the home alarm system, unlocking the double-bolted house door and then the padlock on the gate, locking the door, locking the gate behind me, rushing up the stairs to reach the driveway where my car was parked, removing another padlock and unwrapping the chain that secured the razor-wire gate, sliding back the bolt, releasing the latch, opening the gate, entering my car, driving out of the gate, stepping out of the car, bolting and locking the gate, getting back into the car, and speeding off into the lifeless night.

Every single one of these steps amplified the danger of being accosted by an enterprising moonlighter ready to put a gun to my head, unburden me of my wallet, relieve me of my car, or, worse still, force me back into my home—the consequences of which I shudder to contemplate.

At the bullet-pierced road sign, I made a sharp left turn. The first set of traffic lights glowed red. With the keen eye of an owl on a moonless night, I scanned the intersection and noticed that all was clear. Pressing down on the accelerator with a young man's verve, I approached the next traffic light. It too remained stuck on red, but a white Toyota HiAce prevented me from repeating the maneuver. I came to a halt and left enough space for a hasty escape in case another vehicle tried to wedge me in. I entered the swirl of the on-ramp and continued on in this freewheeling culture that wasn't entirely compliant with the law.

Mr. Singh was there to meet me at the roadside on Clare Road. There was a huge 'For Sale' sign affixed to the gate. He went through the familiar process of unlocking and locking all over again. He reassured me that the rottweiler was safely locked up in the front before directing me to the back entrance of the house.

Mrs. Singh lay curled up, writhing in pain, her body contorted by the sudden attacks of colic and spasms that were linked to her ovarian cysts. The most excruciating episodes occurred just before a cyst was about to rupture.

I prepared a syringe, carefully measuring out pethidine and sparine, a combination that works wonders in alleviating both the pain and the accompanying nausea. The injection provided miraculous relief, allowing Mrs. Singh to find comfort and gradually drift off to sleep. With her condition stabilized, Mr. Singh and I slipped quietly out into the backyard.

It was five in the morning, the flush of dawn, and I found myself standing with Mr. Singh in his backyard. We stood above hundreds of shack dwellings (*jondolos*) that were deliriously fashioned from abandoned pieces of wood, discarded sheet-metal scraps, and cardboard scavenged from supermarket dumpsters. Copper wire, harvested from high-voltage rail cables, was whimsically connected to the municipal grid, providing a free source of electricity. "I noticed the 'For Sale' sign. Any luck?" I asked.

"Who will buy my home now?" he said. "With all these *jondolos* around, I won't get half the price. It's funny, you know, but people who have the money to buy this house think it's a chicken coop, and the people in the *jondolos* think it's a palace."

"That's so sad," I said. "It's a problem everywhere now. There's so much crime too."

"Oh, don't talk about crime. It does not make the news headlines, so people don't know the truth, but I've seen this neighborhood change, I've seen it in my own back yard. Look, here is where a *tsotsi* (troublemaker) took down my precast fence. Now any Tom, Dick, or Harry can walk into my yard," he said.

"Even with the dog?"

"They don't care about the dog. They have guns. Once they threatened to poison my dog."

"Have you had any break-ins, Mr. Singh?"

"Four times they've broken in, and that's only in the past year. They do it in broad daylight now. The police do nothing, so there's no point in even reporting it."

"I'm sorry that you're in this situation," I said.

"What can we do? The ANC promised African people a million houses in one year, but they failed them. All these people came from the farms looking for the houses they were promised. They filled every empty space they could find. Just look at how people in the *jondolos* live."

I said goodbye to Mr. Singh and stood a few moments to look over the *jondolos*. In their outward appearance, they were much like the *favelas* of Rio de Janeiro or the *comunas* of Medellín. The stench of uncollected rubbish filled the air. A scantily-clad young man bathed in the open and rinsed off with a jam tin that he filled with water scooped out of a twenty-five-liter (6.5 gallon) plastic bucket. Curly wisps of smoke rose from an outdoor hearth. A tuck-shop lay nestled among the rows of shacks, with a poorly-scrawled food menu affixed to the corrugated-iron facade. A naked child steered a bare-rimmed bicycle wheel with a stick, sending clucking chickens scattering.

As I drove back home, I realized that Mr. Singh was correct: the newspapers did not report violence and crime as much; and indeed crime had become our constant companion. Now that we had two young children, we needed to find some place that was safer, and away from the shacks.

My dream of living in a house with panoramic views of the ocean had driven me to buy a plot of land—freshly cleared of sugarcane and with a full forty-four-meter frontage—on Herwood Drive in the prime location of Umhlanga Rocks. It boasted unrivaled ocean views, which extended all the way to the Golden Mile on Durban's beachfront. After considering the possibility that *jondolos* might be built alongside, I abandoned that dream and sold the land. It was much safer to buy in a gated community.

In April of 1995, one year after the first democratic elections, we moved into our new home, on Ryder Drive, in the Mount Edgecombe Country Club Estate (MCCE).

MCCE was about ten kilometers north of Durban, and built along the fairways of a golf course. Mount Edgecombe was the place of my father's birth, and our family's home during indenture. The barracks were no more, but it was with triumphant defiance that I came to live right next door to the colonial-styled house that had once belonged to the sugar baron who held dominion over my family when they were indentured laborers. I could not resist the provocative idea of the descendant of a slave living side by side, as an equal, with the descendant of a former master.

Inside the estate we could live in relative freedom, and without the need for home alarm systems and burglar bars on the windows.

Electrified razor-wire fencing secured the perimeter, and access was controlled by entrance gates manned by security personnel, day and night. Our children played on the manicured lawns, and we went for long walks along the tree-lined pathways that led to gently-sloping greens and gleaming white gazebos, overlooking nesting great egrets and frolicking fountains. Our concerns now centered around the mischievous monkeys that darted in through our open windows to snatch bananas off the dining-room table, leaving the ceramic centerpiece shattered on the terracotta-tiled floor.

Living on a stockaded estate did not spare me from the reality of life on the outside. Each time I left our sanctuary—for work, school, shopping, family, or friends—I was confronted by the dangers that lurked outside: gold *thali* chains ripped off married women's necks, cars broken into in broad daylight, shop owners robbed at gunpoint, homes invaded, occupants gagged and bound while their home was ransacked, carjackings, hijackings of cash in transit vehicles, and rape.

On a weekday in July or August of 1995, at around two in the afternoon, the clouds drifted swiftly across the path of the sun. Suddenly, day appeared to turn into night, and the crows, their sensory beacons confused, flew off to roost in the trees. It felt as though the inauspicious shadow of an eclipse had fallen over Hillcrest and portended some grave misfortune. Soon after the re-emergence of the light, I received a call from my wife, Adashnee.

"You need to come quickly," she said.

As much as I protested, she refused to say why.

A flood of grim images rushed through my mind. Had something dreadful befallen one of our children? Tharuna and Kavi were notorious for their pranks, often pretending to choke on Smarties candy. However, the tone of Adashnee's voice indicated that it wasn't about the kids. If it had been, she would have been too overwhelmed to make the call. Perhaps Dad's streak of luck had come to an end, the years of heavy smoking finally taking their toll. Recent silent heart-attacks had left him ineligible for bypass surgery. I envisioned him struggling in the store adjacent to my clinic, grappling with a heavy crate of milk cartons, only to be overwhelmed by agonizing chest-pain before collapsing onto the floor. But perhaps I was allowing my imagination to run wild, and the situation wasn't as sinister as my fears suggested. It could have been a break-in at the clinic, a more plausible explanation. With that thought in mind, I raced back.

When I got there, I found Ama trembling and Dad drawing hard on a cigarette. It took a while for them to regain their composure.

Over the past couple of days, Dad had noticed two young African men watching the shop. Given the prevalence of crime in our area, the thought that they were planning some mischief might have crossed his mind. However, he could not have drawn such a conclusion, not without more tangible evidence.

"Because they were young, and African, did not mean that they were planning a crime," Dad said in a tone of quiet resignation.

"It was around eleven in the morning, and the shop was empty," Dad said. The quieter the place was, the more my parents felt uneasy about strangers. When the two men entered, Dad was at the back, restocking the shelves. At first, they pretended to be ordinary customers.

Suddenly, one of them hopped over the counter and held a switch-blade to Ama's neck. Dad heard the commotion and rushed forward but he was powerless. One of the robbers directed Dad to empty out the cash register into a canvas bag. Then he was forced to fill another bag with cartons of cigarettes that he hastily pushed off the shelves. The men fled into the bushes across the road and down a path that led towards the Old North Coast Road.

Ama was still quivering, her face pale and fearful, but she had settled enough that she could speak. "When he jumped over and asked me not to scream, my life flashed before me. Those five minutes seemed to be unending, I seemed to be living through so many lives. All I wished for, Krish, was that God would ensure that it was quick, that I would not suffer," she said.

Yet, when he held the knife to her throat, when the danger was most intense, a strange calm came over her, as though all her fears had been lifted.

"Now that it is over, everything keeps replaying in my mind, and I'm shaking again."

The police had come and gone. They had followed their usual protocol: scribbling notes, looking for clues, taking fingerprints, handing out a case number, and promising to get back to us. The police were in an endless struggle to impose order on the chaos of our everyday experience. Poor funding had decimated their ranks, and public trust in their roles had been eroded. We did not expect them to find the perpetrators.

"What will come of the police investigation? It's a distortion, a perversion of justice," Dad said.

"We need to settle down, take things easy for a while," I said.

Dad was in a pensive state. "Even if they were found, nothing much would come of it," he said. "Why, even murderers are getting away with pleading poverty nowadays. How irrelevant it is to steal money, or cigarettes, or even hold a knife to someone's neck."

"But crimes just as dreadful, and probably more horrible, have occurred before apartheid ended," I said.

"That is where you're mistaken, Krish, and it's an extremely natural mistake," said Dad. "There is a great difference between criminals of old and this new kind of criminal."

"Crime is crime, Dad. They are all equally culpable," I said.

He banished that thought without even an instant's deliberation.

"In the past, even those criminals, even hardened criminals who showed no remorse, knew that they were *criminals*; they acknowledged the wickedness of their ways. Today, those who commit crimes do not admit that they are criminals at all. Why, some even believe they have a right to do such things," said Dad.

Later that evening, I pondered two things that Dad had mentioned: "Even murderers are getting away without punishment" and "Criminals of today are different."

The counsel for these young perpetrators of crime would admit those facts that can't be avoided. They would have sought other explanations, based on the most liberal, most humane and enlightened view. An extraordinary and convincing plea would be put forward: that these were honest men, whose innocence was injured by poverty or some other societal prejudice, that the need to steal had come *naturally* into their heads. All that would cast their misdeed in an entirely different light. Criminals were indeed getting away with murder.

As busy as I was, I would never miss a James Bond movie and definitely not the weekly episodes of *Colombo* on television. My heroes existed in different worlds, and though each was flawed, every one of them ended up doing the right thing for the right reason. They would not think twice about risking their own safety to rescue others. I realized that Dad was right: that our world was filled with anti-heroes, disenchanted African youth mainly, who thought of themselves as heroes even though they appeared to hold a sense of grievance against society, and were driven to subvert it in the most violent ways. These perpetrators of crime were liberated from the line in the sand that holds the rest of us back, and were not afraid to do horrible things, and to do them without apology.

Two years later, in early December of 1997, I had finished work at my practice in Hillcrest, and made my way to the rooftop parking lot. As I reached into my pockets and wrestled for my keys, I realized that my car was nowhere to be found. Perhaps I had parked on the street, I thought; I often did when I was running late. Slowly, that sinking feeling of unease took root. I stood dazed in the middle of the car park, seized by disbelief, not knowing where I was, or which way I was going.

Confronting the reality that my car had been stolen was as unsettling as it was difficult to accept. I had harbored a misguided belief that I was immune to such misfortune, that I was protected by some armor-plated mantle. Now I, too, had become a victim of crime. Any illusions that I might have had were shattered, and I was forced to face my own vulnerability.

The police called a week later. That was quite a surprise. They informed me that my car had been discovered, abandoned on a remote rural road in Umbumbulu, approximately seventy kilometers away from Hillcrest. I pictured my white 5-Series BMW—the one in which we had brought our newborns, Tharuna and Kavi, home from the hospital—waiting at the side of the road, ready for me to drive off.

Dad drove me down to the spot where the police had located the car. There were fresh signs of damage: tire marks at the edge of the tarmac, the scuffs where the undercarriage was dragged across rocks, and flattened shrubs through which the car had careered. I found her lying beside a thornbush in the ditch, like an animal, full of scrapes and bruises. The roof of my car was crumpled, its once sleek exterior now marred by mud-splattered wheels and deep dents, the paintwork bearing the scars of its unwelcome journey. Inside, the black leather seats were smeared with pasty brown sand. I felt violated, as though a part of me had been breached. All I hoped was that the car was not salvageable, that I would never have to drive it again.

There are things much worse than having one's car stolen, but the burden that crime brought upon us appeared to be cumulative. It slowly chipped away at my confidence, eroded my belief in a law that was intended to protect those who were innocent. It did not help when the police informed me that a few misdirected juveniles were responsible for the theft, that my loss was for the benefit of a mere joyride, and that the culprits were released without censure.

Three months later, on a muggy February afternoon in 1998, I returned from Hillcrest to start work at the practice in Redhill. A murmuring crowd had gathered on the sidewalk opposite my practice. There was a mixture of anguish and anger in their expressions.

"Oh my God, how sad! Those murderous bastards!"

A tall woman, with a kerchief on her head, informed me that an elderly lady had been murdered.

I paused for a moment and looked about, hoping to find any signs that could shed light on the crime that had taken place. Then a policeman stepped forward and moved people to create a path for me to get to the front. Though it might have been futile, there was an expectation for a doctor to do something decisive.

"Down that way," he said.

I was gripped by a dreadful and chilling sense of fear as I made my way along the winding dirt track that led to a clearing among the mango trees. I came upon an old house of wood and iron that stood in a pleasant little garden full of flowers. The entrance was concealed by foliage, the windows shuttered, and freshly laundered linen was hanging out to dry on a line outside. Yellow police tape cordoned off the perimeter of the yard.

I was certain that I heard a muffled sob. As I approached, I saw a young lady standing beside a policeman, and I immediately recognized her as one of my patients. She had the look of a person who had just lost someone. It wasn't just the tears streaming down her cheeks, her quivering lips, or the kohl-rimmed eyes that smudged lines of distress on her face. There was that vulnerability, the raw helplessness of someone wrestling with the profound pain and anguish that accompanies grief.

She remained motionless at first, and then slowly, gravely drifted downwards onto her knees. I took her hand and knelt beside her. With my head bowed, I kept seeking words of comfort, but they remained only as thoughts that were stuck in my mind. It took great effort for her, too, before she finally uttered a few words.

"Why? Why did they have to do this to my child?"

"Good Heavens! *Child. What child*," I exclaimed.

The policeman cleared his throat. "An old lady was raped and then murdered, and the child who was in her care was stabbed to death," he said.

The scale of the distraught young woman's private suffering, though impossible to grasp, was now clear from such a public display of grief. Her desperation was truly heartbreaking: but what does one say to a mother so devastated? How does one comprehend the incomprehensible, or console that which is inconsolable?

The four-year-old—who had been left in the care of the elderly lady while his mother went to work—was the same age as my son, Kavithan. The child who was dead had the most haunting and compelling eyes, eyes that followed my every move whenever I examined him. I remember giving him an injection once, and he looked at me, pierced me with the silence of those beseeching eyes. Now, all I could do was to exhume the memory of a little boy who lay in a pool of blood, those imploring eyes fixed, motionless, and wide.

When adults talk about mortality, we think not of ourselves, not of our own mortality, but that of our children. The loss of a child is against the natural order of things, something that we least expect, what we fear most, and hold at the comfortable distance of denial. It could so easily have been one of our own children. They were playing outside, no more than a hundred meters away. I could not imagine what was flashing through the young mother's mind, but I could perceive it in the context of our own children: the carefully folded christening dress that conjures up the immense joy that comes with the birth of a child, the beaming smiles in the first birthday photographs on the mantelpiece, and the cuddly Teletubby toy lying abandoned on the floor. I was reminded as well about the responsibility we assume to protect our children from harm, harm that is sometimes beyond our intervention.

Truth may be elusive, but our experience is real, and it forces us to think, to argue, and to change. In the aftermath of that tragedy, *our* world had changed, and the composure of *our* lives was destroyed. Everyone has a breaking point, a point of no return. How much was too much? How long was too long? How much more could I endure?

CHAPTER 18

Canada Calls

In the months following those reprehensible murders, a fog had fallen upon me and wrapped me in a dreary solitude. I could not escape that. There were moments, hours, perhaps even whole days, when I was clearly off course, pacing about and doing my best to avoid confronting the full and clear understanding of my position. The previous two years had worn me down. Impulse and instinct had replaced rational thought. Fear does that, and it must have taken immense fear for me to even contemplate leaving the country of my birth.

I chose not to replace the car that was stolen, and opted to buy a second-hand jalopy. Every day that I drove that clunker I felt tormented by a strange self-loathing. When the heart of a man is troubled, he resorts to unimaginable conduct, even deliberately inflicting suffering onto himself, as though to atone for some misdeed.

Early in March of 1998, I played in a fundraising golf tournament at the Mount Edgecombe Country Club. Following a day of golf, I invited my playing partners to join me for drinks at my home.

We sat on our front porch, in the shade of giant jacarandas, chatting and sipping mocktails. In the course of our conversation that evening, one of my medical colleagues told us about his plans to emigrate to Canada. He was moving to Newfoundland that August.

"There is a recruitment event at the Elangeni Hotel next Saturday," he said. "What do you have to lose. Check it out."

Adashnee and I had entertained the idea of emigrating. We had the occasional conversation about the countries where our medical degrees would be recognized. We would talk about how similar the weather was in Australia, the breathtaking natural beauty of New Zealand, and the challenging winters in Canada. I had a preference for Canada. The time I had spent in New York provided a glimpse of life in North America. However, the idea of actually relocating never took root. Despite the pervasive violence and crime that surrounded us, the thought of leaving our families behind in South Africa was too traumatic to contemplate.

The information session at the Elangeni was organized by Canada Calls, a rather enchanting name for a recruitment agency. They extolled the virtues of Canada's public health system, placing the emphasis on work-life balance. They showcased images of the Niagara Falls, the picturesque lakes and evergreen forests in the Canadian Shield, and the vibrant cityscapes in Toronto and Vancouver.

None of those pictures impressed me. I preferred not to set myself up for failure. I had lived in East Marion, a rural part of New York State, and that was just perfect for me. My mood was such that any safe place would have been good enough. What do we have to lose? We'll make it work no matter where we go, I told myself. At the very least it would be an adventure with the kids. Finally, I would get to see Winnipeg and Kicking Horses Pass, places on the Canadian Pacific Railway route that I had studied in geography class at primary school.

Following the presentation, Adashnee was more receptive to the idea of moving to Canada. The weather remained a concern.

"Don't worry, we'll adjust to the winters," I told Adashnee.

All that remained was the difficult task of convincing our parents.

The following day I mustered the courage to talk to my parents about emigrating. The subject weighed heavily on me. Each time I tried to introduce the matter, I descended into a state of agitation, hesitating, procrastinating. I had twisted myself into such a knot that I began to believe that it was best to say nothing, forget it all, and uproot this idea from my memory.

"Something seems to be bothering you, son? Why do you look so troubled?" Dad asked.

"I've always been honest with you, Dad, but this is too difficult to talk about," I said.

"What is it, son?"

He was patient enough to not insist upon an answer. There was silence for a few moments.

I gazed at him gloomily, "Dad, for a long time now, I've been meaning to talk to you about the idea of emigrating. Each time I have held back because it feels like I'm running away, that I'm abandoning you all."

He sat a while and reflected. I noticed how much older he appeared now, how grey and unruly his eyebrows had become. But Dad's mind was still as sharp as ever.

"More recently, Ama and I have been thinking about such things," he said. "Our days are over. There is not much for us to hope for. But you are in a different situation. There is life waiting for you. What you need more than anything is certainty, an atmosphere of calm, a place where you can raise your children in safety. If that is what Adashnee and you have decided, then go with all our blessings."

I was stunned by his response, unable to grasp the magnitude of his compassion. It tormented me even more that he endorsed everything without the slightest disagreement.

"Dad, Canada is so far away, a full twenty-four hours' flying time," I said.

"Perhaps no one will see you for a long time? So, what about it? Everyone is busy with their own lives. Think of it as an adventure into a new world, and when you do come back, think about how much more meaningful those visits would be."

A few weeks later, Canada Calls presented us with job opportunities in Winkler, Manitoba. Later that evening, after accounting for the eight-hour time difference, I called the manager at the Winkler Clinic.

"Will you be able to come at short notice?" he asked. "I can start the process of applying for work permits immediately."

"Mr. Fraser, it would make sense for us to arrive in the summer. We'll need time to adjust gradually before winter comes," I said.

The thought of how much we had to accomplish in such a short time made me delirious and dizzy. There were evaluating exams to write, additional acute-care courses to complete, a clinical rotation in psychiatry to arrange, numerous medical examinations to undergo, and triple-checking of the dates, addresses, and spelling on the immigration forms. Furthermore, we had to wind down our current medical practices, sell our home, address tax and legal matters, and arrange for the shipment of our furniture.

I was thirty-five years old and in the process of undoing my existing world. Starting all over again was disconcerting. Yet somehow I tried to make peace with my situation. During the early mornings, I went for long walks along the beach, quite forgetting where I was at times. I watched the soothing rush of waves gently lapping onto the shore, the salty tang filling the air, and the white foamy peaks brushing against my feet. I looked up at the fluffy cloud formations, imagining them to be French poodles. On weekends, we went out for lunches and sat on café patios that overlooked the ocean in Umhlanga. I found myself chewing slowly and deliberately, watching the oddities of passers-by, observing an African Monarch butterfly feeding off milkweed, talking about intention and fate, and arguing that everything happens for a reason.

I wanted to be alone, alone and in a silent place, so that I could contemplate the turn my life had taken.

In my mind's eye, I began to see the outline of the precipitous cliffs that make up the Amphitheatre in the Drakensberg Mountains, and especially a certain spot at the source of the Tugela River, which I used to frequent. In this place, with time my sole contemporary, I looked around me at a world that was summit and abyss both together, and I imagined myself looking up into the heavens and bargaining. I wished that all of this was just a silly dream, a state of delirium. Perhaps I would snap out of it and realize that everything was fine; that this was merely an illusion.

Alas! It was not a dream, and before I could fully comprehend my situation, it was time to go.

CHAPTER 19

A Child of the Universe

You may not have noticed the anguish in my soul, or the profound helplessness that accompanied my decision to leave the land of my birth. I found myself wearing the expression of a man walking the plank, torn to the core by the conflicting imperatives of self-interest and allegiance to my country. It is all too convenient to oversimplify our history by reducing it to choices between loyalty and betrayal, heroes and traitors, or those who stay and those who leave. It is easier to assign labels and slot people into categories, to deny the emotional trauma that underlies the choices we make.

Despite everything, I wanted to stay and help save the country that I still loved. But I was no longer sure that my country loved me back, or even what my country *was* anymore.

Each of us has his or her own jealously-guarded hopes and motivations, and must find a way through the unmarked paths of a complicated world. My decision to leave, in search of a better life, was influenced by deeply personal circumstances. Yet it was no easy decision to renounce the place that has been home to a lifetime of memories. I would miss the warm summers and mild winters, the ships dotting the horizon across an azure-blue ocean, the rolling hills of sugarcane, and the lavender bursts of jacarandas. Perhaps those could easily be replaced, but who would fill the void of the people who had become a part of my existence?

The thought of leaving behind my family and friends weighed heavily upon me. They were the people whom I had grown up with and come to love, people who could vouch for the person that I am. I was surrendering the simplicity and certainty of all those relationships, and resigning myself to a future in which I would have to forge a fresh path, and rely on memory to provide that thread of continuity in my life.

On the last day of June of 1998, our bags were packed, and we were ready to go. Throughout the morning, John Denver's refrain ran like an incantation: "Don't know when I'll be back again."

I lay in bed, flipping through postcards of the Golden Mile, that glamorous stretch of Durban's beachfront lined with fancy hotels and restaurants. The Golden Mile held a treasure-trove of memories, reminders of my family's life of indenture, our ambitious nature, and the pettiness of racism. It reminded me of fond childhood memories, now tarnished by crime and my vulnerability in South Africa. Above all, it brought me to a different understanding of what it means to belong.

In the first picture, the cannons—placed at Battery Beach by the British during World War II—can be seen, with their barrels pointing out to sea.

Over a hundred years ago a ship dropped anchor in the waters opposite Battery Beach. It was low tide, and a sandbar blocked its entry into the harbor. The ship, awaiting the next high tide, was the *SS Congella*, and on board was my great-grandfather. The cannons reminded me about our colonial past, and the Empire that conspired to commit my family to a foreign land.

Like first-generation immigrants the world over, my family faced significant challenges while trying to establish a life in their new country. Their determination to succeed led them to work tirelessly, and to prioritize their children's education. Each generation made sacrifices to ensure that their children would have better prospects. To this day, there are many who consider us outsiders in South Africa. The uncertainty of our position creates an anxiety, a tension that makes us continue to strive as though we were still first-generation immigrants.

Is it a flaw to be driven by this kind of ambition, one fueled by the certainty that education and hard work can be rewarding? After all, it is this conviction that has lifted my family from a life of labor on the sugarcane fields, and has sustained us through the generations.

In the second postcard, concrete piers can be seen jutting out into the ocean. They are the only artificial divisions in an otherwise endless stretch of golden sand. I look more closely, searching for the restrictive racial signs that separated the shoreline during apartheid. They are all gone now. I see Black children frolicking in the paddling pools opposite the Elangeni Hotel. The legs that dangle from the ski-lifts are in shades that are more reflective of a society freed from racial segregation.

That picture reminds me of an age of innocence, a time when I perceived the world around me in ways that adults may overlook, paying attention to subtle changes in body language, and having an intuitive sense, even though no words were spoken. I am reminded as well about the damaging encounters that initiated me into a racially-segregated reality: the humiliation of being squashed into a third-class coach when others were vacant, the ridicule of being called a 'Coolie,' and the unearned hostility from an angry woman who wanted me to go back where I came from.

We are not born with discrimination in our hearts. The intentional divisions imposed during apartheid were intended to stop us from seeing the humanity that we shared with others. It is disheartening to recall my childhood fear of African people, and the way they were portrayed as intimidating figures of apprehension and mistrust.

During that time, I saw myself solely as a victim of prejudice, a Brown person discriminated against by White people in apartheid South Africa. I failed to acknowledge the ways in which my own family inadvertently perpetuated racism: our obsession with skin-lightening creams, the lengths we went to in avoiding exposure to the sun, the Indian films we watched that portrayed only fair-skinned people as heroes, and dark-skinned people as villains. I think about the derogatory names we attributed to teachers who didn't win our favor, like 'Black Botie' and 'Zulu.' My conscience was comfortably nestled in the guise of victimhood; yet I have come to recognize that none of us is above racism.

The next postcard captures the essence of the late 1970s. It showcases the grandeur of the Maharani Hotel, which, true to its name, reigned as the queen of luxury. On the outside walls of the Maharani is an elevator, pictured as it moves upwards towards the Raffles Nightclub at the top of the hotel, while a row of gleaming cars lines the street outside.

I recall the wonder and enchantment that I felt as a child, our family strolling along the Golden Mile on a hot summer's evening, under a night of stars, with a cool breeze blowing over the ocean, and the air filled with the aroma of seafood sizzling on the grill.

It has all become so tainted now, those fond memories clouded over by a fog of fear and uncertainty. In my childhood, I hadn't seen anything so spectacular as the elevator on the outside of the Maharani. The magic was gone, the memory of the elevator stripped of its allure. Perhaps it was the faded nostalgia of a bygone era, when I was not burdened by any responsibility, when life was more predictable, and I felt more secure.

My gaze wanders across the cars depicted on the postcard, and my thoughts shift to the present. I envision a spark-plug flung through the side window of a sleek, new Mercedes Benz. The sound of the car alarm pierces the air, followed by a hot-wired ignition. The vehicle screeches away towards a chop-shop located beyond the city limits. In my mind's eye, I see the identification number being removed from the engine block. A fresh coat of paint is sprayed on, and there's a rapid change of registration plates. Yet, amidst this vivid imagery, not a single person turns around to witness the theft. This is how we live now, with crime that has become all too commonplace. People have resigned themselves to the futility of it all. They simply continue on their way, unaffected by the scene of a crime unfolding before them.

I live in a world in which AK-47 automatic rifles are ordinary articles, a place where bank robberies, home invasions, and carjackings constantly occupy my mind. The real culprits roam freely, while the innocent are confined behind windows reinforced with burglar bars, double-gated doors, and barbed-wire perimeters.

The relentless grip of crime and violence forces me to ponder our hard-fought political freedom. We earned the right to vote and elect our own leaders, and they promised a "better life for all." But our new-found democracy is losing its way. I feel deeply disappointed that just as I was beginning to grasp the essence of belonging to South Africa, it is not politics or economics, but the pervasive nature of crime, that is forcing me out.

I want to accept all of these things as the necessary elements of restoring justice in a fledgling democracy: the cost of rebalancing political power, reallocating resources, and redressing social inequalities. However, I feel the desperation of a shipwrecked sailor. How I wish that I could stuff a message of hope into a glass bottle and toss it into the sea opposite the Maharani. Maybe, just maybe, some trident-bearing celestial hero would stumble upon my plea, and rescue us from the tempest that is ripping through our country.

In the following postcard, at Addington Beach, on the southern end of the Golden Mile, a seagull gracefully soars in a gentle arc above a solitary Indian fisherman. The man battles to hold on to his fishing rod, while the vast ocean looms menacingly, as if ready to engulf him.

The scene captures so vividly the threats that are echoed by African maids who work in Indian households. They warn that Indian people will be cast into the ocean, the very place from where our ancestors had come, and the place where we really belong. It is, after all, the *Indian* Ocean.

Those kinds of threats make me feel vulnerable, an Indian person caught in the middle, between Black and White. During apartheid, I experienced discrimination for not being White enough. Despite identifying with the Black cause and contributing to our liberation from apartheid, I now find myself in a position where I am not Black enough. The plight of the Indian fisherman makes me wonder how it happened that I find myself in such a precarious position in South Africa.

During apartheid, as an Indian person I was perceived to be the 'better' non-White. I attended better schools, and the government provided me with free textbooks. People in my family were more educated, and held better jobs. They were teachers and managers in factories; and even if they drove delivery vehicles, they were spared from the physically-demanding tasks of moving heavy loads. Whether it was construction work, gardening, or maid services, we enlisted cheap African labor that spared us from physical strain. Consequently, I cannot ignore the reality that my privileged position to some extent benefited from the labor of African people. This perception of us as the 'better non-White' has caused African people to look upon us as exploitative individuals who flourished in our roles as 'non-White masters.'

In moments of quiet contemplation, I acknowledge the pride and exclusivity by which I have come to see myself as better. I have no tribal status in South Africa, and no claim to any ancestral land; therefore I am driven by ambition, and have anchored my life with an emphasis on education. This has unfortunately contributed to a culture that makes others appear lazy. This regrettable set of circumstances has created a divide between individuals like me, and those who have experienced a more challenging and disadvantaged past.

In my childhood, and throughout my youth, the term 'existential threat' was not one that I was familiar with. The sense of urgency that it conveys, the flavor of darkness that it invokes, captures for me the collective vulnerability of Indian people in South Africa. Sometimes, when I lie in bed, I find myself contemplating doomsday scenarios: an asteroid crashing into Earth, a super volcano exploding over Yellowstone National Park, or our planet being sucked into the cosmic abyss of a black hole. None of these thoughts keep me awake at night.

Indian people did not have silver spoons in their mouths, or money-trees in their yards; yet I think about the slippery ways that people misconstrue our success as elitism or exploitation. I fear that it would not take much for some crazy, maverick politician to trip an explosion, and the unthinkable act of genocide could easily become the inevitable. It is this that keeps me up at night.

The last postcard depicts the expanse of a fathomless ocean. It makes me feel like I am standing on the precipitous edge of the world, over the vastness of a whole new frontier, a gateway to unchartered territories and endless possibilities. It feels as though I belong in two different dimensions now, inhabiting two worlds at once.

I leave behind a world that is filled with fond memories, but one in which I have lost hope. Hope dies all the time, but we must believe that it will be rekindled and sustained by a renewed purpose. If this hope was not a possibility for myself, then at least I wished that our children would discover that the world is wider than they could imagine, and that they could access the freedom to move comfortably between countries and continents. Above all, I trusted that they would gain a sense of belonging to their new country.

I imagine standing on the edge of this new frontier, surveying the immensity of what lies ahead. My quest to experience life from a different vantage-point exposes me to the anxiety of resettlement in a world yet unborn. I wonder if the best is over, and whether that which lies on the other side is only to be endured. There is no guarantee that a life in Canada will give me the sense of connectedness and kinship that I am leaving behind, no guarantee that I would not face racism and alienation.

As uncertain as my future appeared, I felt empowered by a newfound conviction. I have finally transcended my narrow view of belonging. No matter where I am, I will hold onto the idea that I am one with the Universe: mingling amongst the stars in the night sky, gliding along in the depths of the ocean, and scaling the tops of the highest mountains. I belong in Africa, in Asia, and in the Americas, as much as I do in Europe and at the polar caps of the Arctic and Antarctic. Perhaps this sounds delusional: but deep inside I feel a spiritual sense of connectedness, a cosmic force that binds me to everything. It is this belief that gives renewed purpose and meaning to my life.

I spent the rest of the morning pushing the limits of time, hoping that I could postpone the inevitable. Before I realized it, I was handing the airline agent our one-way tickets. I watched as she weighed our bags, all eight of them, before she handed me the boarding passes. It was time for us to bid our final goodbyes.

I wrapped my arms around Ama, aware that she must be enduring even greater pain than I was. Her hair was impeccably arranged (as usual), her face made up, and a red teardrop dot adorned her forehead. However, the vibrant cerise lipstick which usually emphasized a smile stretching from cheek to cheek had lost its shine.

At first, she struggled to find her voice. Then, with a noticeable tremor in her tone, she said, "Don't worry about us. We'll be fine. Take care of the children."

I embraced Dad. It shocked me to see that my father's eyes were glistening with tears. It was only in the last few years that we had become comfortable with sharing our innermost feelings. I was going, and he was seeing me go. It came to me as never before, and now his tears were saying it. He loved me.

Seeing Dad respond in this way made me realize that I might never see him again. In those fleeting seconds of our embrace, time stretched out, like a suspended moment, poised on the edge of anticipatory grief. I envisioned that dreaded phone call in the middle of the night, myself as a trembling exile who hastily boards a plane and returns to this very place, like a timid child, coming to bid my final farewell.

I could not find the words to convey to my parents how much they meant to me, how their unwavering support had shaped my life, and how much I loved them. Those things that were beyond words remained unreleased in my mind, and lingered only in tear-filled glances and in tight embraces.

We passed through the security gates. We were alone now and enveloped in a somber silence. Even at this late hour, I wished with all my heart that it did not have to be this way. My teary gaze fell upon Adashnee and our children. They were the future I had to protect.

My thoughts drifted once more to my great-grandfather as he stood on the gangway in Madras a century ago and looked out at the land that he was leaving forever. Did he utter a silent prayer? Did he see fleeting visions of his parents, his friends, the religious festivals, and life in the village that were his anchor? Was there a hint of sadness—for surely, he would have missed it all?

Similar emotions were now flashing through my mind—a mixture of sadness, excitement, adventure, and uncertainty all rolled into one. There was no magical solution, only a lifelong journey that had to be taken one step at a time. The choices we make, the decisions we take, are never so clear as black and white, but come in shades that are somewhere in between.

THE END

Kindly consider writing an honest review at:

Goodreads - goodreads.com

or

Amazon - amazon.com

Thank you.

This memoir would not have been possible without the love and support of my family, friends, colleagues and so many others who have contributed to my understanding of the events in my life. I am so thankful to be part of your lives.

I acknowledge the sacrifices that we're made by my indentured ancestors and their generation, their unyielding resilience in the face of insurmountable difficulties in the years during indenture and beyond. I also acknowledge the harm that have befallen those who suffered under a long history of colonialism and racism in South Africa. May we find the strength to reconcile our differences and live in a peaceful society.

My gratitude to my parents for their undying support despite the most trying times in our lives.

I am thankful to the following individuals who helped me shape this story in a meaningful way:

Marion Roach Smith (USA), whose masterclass taught me the nuances of memoir writing.

Lisa Dale Norton (USA) for her developmental editing.

Sarah Chauncey (Canada) for improving my storytelling technique.

Christopher Hoffman (USA) and Brooks Becker(USA) for the copy edits.

Penny Silva(UK) for proofreading the final copy.

Damon Freeman and the team at Damonza (New Zealand), for designing the cover and formatting the book.

I thank the people who gave permission to mention their names in the book and to those who I am unable to name. Thank you all:

Anil Bhoopal

Kidar Ramgobind

Billy Ramakgopa

I thank you, the reader, for taking the time to learn about my life.

Ganesan Abbu is a graduate of the University of Natal Medical School, in Durban, South Africa.

He is a Family Physician in Winkler Manitoba, Professor in the Department of Family Medicine at the University of Manitoba, Canada, and the current President of the Manitoba College of Family Physicians - a chapter of The College of Family Physicians of Canada.

www.ingramcontent.com/pod-product-compliance
Lightning Source LLC
Chambersburg PA
CBHW071422080526
44587CB00014B/1722